6 principles to retire younger & richer

# 6 principles to retire younger & richer

## daniel walsh

MAJOR
STREET

# Acknowledgments

This book is dedicated to the individuals who have played integral roles in my life.

To my beloved wife, Sophie, whose enduring support has been a constant in my life. Even in the face of my wildest ideas, you've been a stabilising force, always there to bring me back to earth while standing by my side.

To my parents, who taught me the value of investment from a young age and instilled in me a strong work ethic. Your guidance and the lessons you imparted have been the bedrock of my journey.

I extend my gratitude to all of you for your consistent support and unwavering faith in me. You have been my inspiration and driving force, and I am deeply thankful for your presence in my life.

Thank you also to Nicola McDougall, a trusted friend from the early days of my first company, whose continuous support and belief in my success have been instrumental in bringing this book to life. Your commitment to this project has been invaluable, and without your partnership I would not have completed it. Thank you for the support and encouragement in getting my thoughts to paper and sharing them with the world.

**MAJOR STREET**

First published in 2024 by Major Street Publishing Pty Ltd
info@majorstreet.com.au | +61 406 151 280 | majorstreet.com.au

 A catalogue record for this book is available
from the National Library of Australia

Printed book ISBN: 978-1-922611-95-6
Ebook ISBN: 978-1-922611-96-3

Cover design by Typography Studio
Internal design by Production Works
Printed in Australia by IVE

10 9 8 7 6 5 4 3 2 1

## Disclaimer

The material in this publication is in the nature of general comment only, and neither purports nor intends to be advice. Readers should not act on the basis of any matter in this publication without considering (and if appropriate taking) professional advice with due regard to their own particular circumstances. The author and publisher expressly disclaim all and any liability to any person, whether a purchaser of this publication or not, in respect of anything and the consequences of anything done or omitted to be done by any such person in reliance, whether whole or partial, upon the whole or any part of the contents of this publication.

# Contents

# Why I can retire at just 32

When I was 19, my mum was diagnosed with stage three breast cancer. It knocked our family for six as the chances of her surviving were slim.

I can still clearly remember the day my parents broke the news to me. Losing my mum, who was only 40, was not something I had ever considered as a young man.

My dad was willing to do anything he could to save the love of his life, including shuttering his auto electrical business if he had to and selling off the real estate assets that they had diligently bought with their hard-earned cash over the years.

I was working as a third-year apprentice for my dad and so was able to keep the business afloat – as best as I could given my young age – while my mum underwent treatment and fought for her life. All of the focus was on saving mum's life, so my parents sold off everything apart from the family home to keep the financial wolf from our door.

Miraculously, my mum survived, but that dreadful disease robbed my parents of a better financial life. In fact, the properties they sold to realise $850,000 in cash back then would be worth $2.5 million today.

Not only did the experience make me never again take my family or my health for granted, it also set me on a path to create a better financial life for my family. From that moment on, I learned everything I could about creating wealth.

I bought my first property when I was 19 and earning just $34,000 a year as an apprentice. I added to my portfolio each year, but I also made other financial investments along the way.

Today, at just 32, I own a $20 million portfolio with my wife Sophie, which has $10 million in equity. My portfolio of assets yields about 7 per cent annually, or about $116,000 every single month. That is more than the average Aussie worker earns in a whole year! At one point I also built up a portfolio of cryptocurrency from $400,000 to more than $1.8 million in just 12 months.

I have created significant wealth when most young people are still pondering whether they can 'afford' to invest in anything at all – and I believe that my success is due to the unique wealth blueprint I have created that features six principles anyone can follow to retire younger and richer. My system will teach you how you can retire at a time and age of your choosing. It will also teach you how to create generational wealth so that your children, and their children (and *their* children), can build on the fruits of your labour long after you are gone.

About now, you're probably thinking that it doesn't seem possible. Perhaps this is because you didn't learn wealth concepts when you were younger, or you struggle to imagine a life where you aren't trading your time for money via wages or even working for yourself in a blue-collar industry as I once did. But believe me, you can change your financial future by following my six principles to retire younger and richer.

I know this for a fact because I did it myself!

## My story

Like all apprentices, my pay was abysmal: I started my auto electrician apprenticeship when I was 16, and my first pay cheque was a paltry $254 per week. But that didn't stop me from investing in my first property by the time I was just 19. As soon as I started working, my mission was to save everything that I could and invest it into property.

I did everything on my own. It took me about four years to save $34,000, which was really tough on apprentice wages, as you can imagine. Every week I would transfer 50 per cent of my wages into an account that I couldn't access. I would carpool to TAFE and work to reduce costs. Unlike my mates, I also didn't spend much time at nightclubs or take overseas holidays. Rather, I opted to live a financially conservative life to achieve my goal of home ownership as soon as possible.

My dedication to creating a better financial future was so strong that when I constructed my first property on a vacant block of land, I had to sell some beloved possessions to complete the project because I still didn't really have enough money. I used to skydive when I was much younger, so I sold my skydiving backpack and my car so I could afford to build the driveway and the fence.

I replaced my car with a $1500 bomb that I drove for two years until it died on the side of the road one day. Before it went completely kaput, it had blown up once before and I had rebuilt the engine. After it blew up again, I sold it for $1500 – the same as I had paid for it.

I had to go from driving a nice car to driving a bomb, but by the time it conked out I owned two houses, so it was clearly worth it. I loved driving the car as well because I knew it was helping me get to my goals – even if some of my friends made fun of me for driving such a piece of junk around.

After finishing my apprenticeship at 20, I decided that there were other careers of interest to me that I could also make more money from and help me with my dream of creating significant wealth while I was still young. I chose to become a freight train driver, which involved a number of years of study.

When I started working on trains, the wages were $750 per week, which was the same as at my last job, but I knew that if I studied for a few years then they would increase a lot more than if I remained an auto electrician. I had placed myself in a better situation so that I could grow my earning capacity faster.

I also kept building my portfolio, courtesy of the equity in my first two properties as well as my clearly superhuman ability to save. I leveraged my first property to buy my second, which I also leveraged to invest in my third property. It had taken me four years to save the deposit for my first property, but I made that back again in equity in just two years' time.

By the time I was working full-time as a freight train driver at 25, I owned six properties. I became a property millionaire not long after, with the equity in my portfolio hitting the magical million-dollar mark.

In 2017, I set up Your Property Your Wealth with my wife Sophie to help people invest in property so they, too, could create wealth. However, I continued to moonlight as a train driver, which literally nearly killed me (a story for later on in this book), until I decided to dedicate my energy solely to the business to assist other young people to get their start in the property market.

I kept adding to my portfolio as well as investing in crypto, and today, at just 32, I could retire and live off the cash flow from investments – but that's not what I want to do at all.

Unlike some other investment books that promote property investing, I don't believe you need 20 or 30 real estate holdings to be 'rich'. Rather, purchasing a smaller number of assets with plenty of capital growth upside is a far more achievable strategy for anyone seeking to retire younger and richer.

So, in this book, I want to teach you everything I have learned during my journey – the good and the bad – to help you achieve your wealth creation goals and dreams through six simple principles. You will also find a number of real-life case studies scattered throughout the book, representing just a small proportion of the people – young and old – who I have helped improve their financial futures and outcomes during my career so far.

## Introduction

# Why most middle-class people will never be rich

Most people trade their time for money, which means they are unlikely to ever create significant wealth. Instead, they should learn how to use their income to buy assets that will increase in value, potentially forever.

Making the jump from working class to middle class is easier than it used to be because of increasing rates of education, including tertiary, as well as baby boomers' property wealth being passed on to their gen X and millennial children. But the transition from middle class to wealthy is a path too long for most people because they generally don't invest in assets that can make them richer, or they don't have the ability to hold these assets over the long term.

The major impediment, though, is that most middle-class people spend their entire working lives trading their time for money via wages or a salary, or being self-employed but never really getting ahead financially to any great degree. This means that the few hours they have left in each working day are spent with friends and family because they don't have the energy to upskill and improve their financial education.

## The big C

My family history is not dissimilar to the scenario I have just described – I had a typical middle-class upbringing. During my childhood and formative years, my parents provided everything that we needed, but they had to trade their time for money to be able to do so. Plus, a big chunk of the household income was spent on bad debt, such as loans for cars and boats.

Don't get me wrong, my upbringing would be classed as above average compared to world standards, because we never had to worry about where our next meal was coming from or be concerned about having a roof over our heads. But if we wanted 'nice things' then my parents had to trade more of their time to make more money to pay for them.

They ran a successful auto electrical business (and still do), which took up more hours each day than a typical nine-to-five job ever would. They worked hard every day, but they also tried to plan for their retirement by buying a couple of investment properties. Then, life happened (as it so often does).

My mum's battle with stage three breast cancer robbed my parents of a better financial life and resulted in them being about $1.7 million worse off. That money would have made a big difference to their twilight years. Of course, we were fortunate that they had assets to sell off at all, because if they hadn't been able to do that, their business would have gone under as well.

While most people will thankfully not experience such a traumatic episode when they are young, this shows how the ability to hold assets for the long term is one of the biggest reasons why some people become rich and some wind up back where they started.

Many in older generations have sold their assets over the years, perhaps to trade up or even because they were scared by one of the dodgy property market forecasts that permeate the media daily. When they do that, though, they soon find that property prices keep rising over time and they are unable to buy a similar property again – or even any property at all.

For those who have been squirrelling their savings away in the bank, well, their money has literally been devaluing over recent years because of record low interest rates and inflation.

In 2023, of course, we saw much higher interest rates than had been common for more than a decade, which was admittedly better for savers, but we also saw property prices continue to rise because of a significant property listing shortage, which prevented many people from entering the market.

## Time for money

Aside from my mum's battle with cancer, the experience of working for my parents – and watching them trade their time for money and come home exhausted at the end of every day – made me dedicate myself to creating a wealthier life while I was still a teenager.

Even before mum became sick, I remember being very angry about how little I was managing to save from my meagre apprentice wages, because I knew I was never going to become richer if I carried on trading my valuable time for not-so-valuable money.

One particular day, my anger boiled over, and I shouted out to my dad that I just wanted to make more money! Well, my dad simply replied that he and my mum had always made more money (via capital growth) by investing in real estate than from their actual business. It was a real lightbulb moment for me!

When I was still at school, my parents would run the business during the week, but at the weekends they would renovate the old properties they had bought and sell them for a healthy profit. They also did some small property developments along the way, which always made them a solid profit.

(Years later, I asked why he was still working, and he said he had to keep working because they had sold their portfolio when mum got sick. None of us have ever regretted that, because it was a necessity, but it set them back years before they could even think about retiring.)

My dad explained to me how they made money from investing by purchasing a property for about $120,000 (it was the 1990s, remember), spending about $30,000 renovating it and then renting it out for about $200 per week. Today, each of those properties would be worth around $800,000 and be bringing in $600 per week or more in rental income.

I absorbed this information like a sponge because finally I could see a path out of the rat race. I didn't need to keep working and working, hoping that one day I would become rich by some mystical magic. No, I started to understand that if I ever wanted to become wealthy, I needed to save enough of my apprentice wages to start buying assets that were likely to increase in value forever.

The path to riches is never easy, nor is it quick. However, I never lost sight of my goal, which was to retire younger and richer than anyone in my family had ever done before.

Back then, like all apprentices, my pay was appalling, but that didn't stop me from investing in my first property before I even hit 20 years of age.

Since that 'lightbulb' conversation with my father all those years ago, my mission has been to save everything that I could and put it into property.

### Investment tip

Over the past decade I have amassed a net worth of $10 million, which equates to $800,000 per year in wealth creation. Looking back, I learned one very valuable lesson: over time, your investments will always outperform your earned income. Therefore, your objective should always be to transfer your hard-earned active income into an asset that will work for you even when you are sleeping.

## Overloaded capacity

Looking back, it is easy to see how most people get stuck on the wage-earning roundabout. Once they finish their apprenticeship or university degree, they start earning money for the first time after having to rely on cash handouts from their parents (if they're lucky) while at high school, and perhaps they promptly decide to spend as much of it as possible! Not only that, but they also use their newfound 'wealth' to apply for credit cards and car loans, which keep them on the debt hamster wheel – potentially for the rest of their lives.

I was lucky because by the time I started working as a freight train driver, I had already decided to dedicate my life to making my income work as hard as possible for me. I had no 'bad debt' as I was driving around in a really crappy car (so, no car loan) and didn't own a credit card.

But it was during my train-driving journey that my commitment to retiring younger and richer really started to build up steam, because I used any downtime I had to educate myself on investment principles. Because I was driving long-distance trains, I usually had several hours free during each journey to dedicate to investment education. My co-driver and I used to take turns driving to prevent fatigue, which usually involved five hours at the helm and five hours off. Some people used their allocated downtime to sleep, which I did sometimes, too, if I needed it, but whenever I could I used those precious hours to study wealth creation techniques and the power of mindset. This is when I learned about the game of property and leverage.

My commitment to my goal was such that I engineered my shifts to complete my weekly allocation of driving time as quickly as possible. This meant I would be rostered on to complete 27 hours of driving in one shift, which necessitated ten hours of driving at night, seven hours when I could sleep while the train was unloaded during the day, then another ten hours driving home that afternoon and into the night. I would then finish around 2 a.m. and drive an hour and a half home to get some sleep. I would complete this in two days, which would give me five days off every week, which I would then use to increase my knowledge even further.

By this stage, I already owned six properties and had started a business, Your Property Your Wealth, to help other people like me build their own property investment portfolios and create long-term wealth. On a typical shift, while my offsider slept during the day, I would jump in a car and drive to the nearest town where there was mobile phone service so I could engage with my burgeoning buyers' agency business. A few hours later, I would drive back to the freight train and drive it home. I was lucky if I slept two hours in every shift, which was just plain silly and reckless in hindsight, but I was willing to do whatever it took to build my wealth.

Many of the other train drivers worked overtime on their days off, so at least I never did that as well. Rather, when I had recovered from my shifts, I would put every waking hour towards studying wealth creation and learning how to exit the rat race as soon as possible.

Deep down, I knew that I didn't want to be working at this job and doing these crazy hours until I was 65, only to retire and die a few years later. I had noticed that in the world of trains and shift work, not many of the guys lived more than about two years after retirement. In fact, there were studies done when I was working there that said the type of shiftwork we did stole an average of 10 years off your life! I couldn't bear the thought of losing a decade of my life, so I set myself a hard deadline of when I would quit and dedicate my life to helping others achieve a wealthier future. I made a commitment to myself: I had 10 years – and not a moment more – to make the money and invest the money so I could retire and get off of the freight-train not-so-merry-go-round.

I did it in nine years – but the road was fairly rocky in hindsight. Somewhere along the way, my dedication to my goal started to become dangerous, because I was trying to do too much with too little time. Something had to give, and it very nearly did in the worst possible way.

Two years before my decade deadline, I thought I was managing to juggle my train-driving career with my small business and my marriage to Sophie reasonably well, but one day the cold hard truth hit me square in the face – literally. Like some kind of maniac, I once did three 27-hour shifts in a row... and 20 minutes after finishing my last shift, and hardly sleeping at all, I fell asleep at the wheel of my car while driving home. The car went through a red light and crashed into another vehicle square on. I hit them at around 70 kilometres an hour. The crash was so bad that the front wheels came off my car. Luckily, everyone walked away from it.

Unsurprisingly, I realised at that moment just how far I had pushed my body and that I was at breaking point. I was never so stupid again and I quit train driving six months later.

## Helping others

I switched my focus to my business, which went from strength to strength quite quickly.

Since 2017, Your Property Your Wealth has helped more than 800 people in Australia purchase an investment property! Our clients have increased their wealth positions by hundreds of thousands of dollars over the years, and some by millions, which makes me a very happy man.

Our property investment strategy involves buying affordable houses that have strong capital growth prospects as well as solid yields. We look for these in blue-collar areas and 'bridesmaid' suburbs next to higher-priced suburbs in both urban and major regional locations around the nation. Most of our clients buy more than one investment property using our service because of our affordable investment strategy, as well as the superior capital growth and cash flow results we have achieved for them.

We experienced outstanding growth in 2021. The total value of properties transacted over the 2020–21 financial year was an extraordinary $138,450,000, which represents 213 properties purchased for 103 clients.

As soon as I exited the train driving business, I kept adding to my portfolio as well as investing in cryptocurrencies, which means that today I could retire at just 32 and live a good life off the income from my investments. But I don't want to retire just yet, even though I easily could. Instead, I want to help as many people as possible achieve the same results as I have. So, rather than retiring after less than 15 years of trading my time for money, I decided to write down all the lessons I have learned – some the hard way – so that everyone has the opportunity to retire younger and richer if they wish to do so.

If you are working or middle class and want to make the leap from working for money to making your money make you more money, the best time to do something about it is right now.

In the next chapter, you will learn the first principle to help you retire younger and richer, which is to build generational wealth. It also touches on how your friends have more to do with your wealth creation than you might think.

## Top 3 takeaways

1. Most people will never be rich because they trade all of their time for money via wages, salary or self-employment.

2. You must learn how to invest your income into assets that will grow in value and make you more money over the decades, even while you sleep.

3. You don't need to own 30 properties to retire younger and richer. It's always about the quality and value of the assets, and *never* the volume.

# Case study

## Developing a wealth creation strategy in your 20s

Josh decided early on that he wanted to create a better financial life for himself because he had watched his parents struggle financially during his upbringing. When he was still in his early 20s, he decided that he needed to start that process and, as luck would have it, happened upon my educational content across social media platforms.

Josh, who is now 28 and an air conditioning mechanic, decided to take his time before reaching out, so he spent the next year or two learning about property investment from my content online as well as saving hard for a deposit. In 2019, he felt educated and confident enough to make contact, and by August that year I had helped the Brisbane-based tradie purchase a house in Geelong for $387,000 that went on to increase in value by 67 per cent over three years.

Josh benefitted not only from the capital growth but also because I helped him buy the property for a discount as a result of some water issues that were identified in the building and pest inspection report.

'After it settled, Dad and I flew down and had a look, because my dad is a tradie too,' Josh recalls. 'We actually found that all the pipes for the stormwater that was coming off the house had been damaged by tree roots through the front of the garden. So, we dug all that up and replaced it – problem solved.'

The strong results from his first investment, and the trust he had in me, meant Josh was keen to add to his portfolio within a year, even though the COVID-19 pandemic had just started and many people at the time were unnecessarily worried about future market conditions.

'I always looked at the long term, so I was never worried about it, and Daniel always had the positive outlook that the pandemic was never going to have a negative impact on the market. The way he explained it, it just resonated – it made so much sense,' he says.

In November of that year, Josh settled on a house in northern Brisbane for $410,000, which increased in value by nearly 60 per cent ($240,000) over the next two years.

Two strategically selected investment properties in two years had resulted in Josh's equity soaring, so he decided to purchase a third property, this time in the eastern suburbs of Brisbane. That property was purchased for $550,000 in September 2021 and achieved capital growth of $120,000 over the next 14 months.

So, within the space of just three years, Josh's property wealth had increased by a staggering $632,000, or $210,000 per year – far more than he could earn as a tradie in the same period.

It certainly seems that Josh is well on his way to achieving his goal of creating a better financial future for himself – and he's not done yet. Over the next few years, Josh wants to buy a home and more investments – he is currently a rentvester – and is also considering diversifying into commercial property.

'Over the next 20 years or so, I want to just keep maximising my results in a safe way,' Josh says. 'My goal is just to keep going, keep maximising my debt while I'm still so young, and trying to use that in my favour.

'When you talk with Daniel, it's like talking to your mate versus talking to someone who's out there trying to take every bottom dollar from you. Daniel cares so much. Every property that he's helped me purchase is similar to a property he's purchased for himself. It's clear from my history, from my three or four years with him so far, how well I have done. And now some of my friends are working with Daniel and have done well themselves.'

## Principle 1

# Build generational wealth

Generationally wealthy families dominate the financial news stories. Just think of the Waltons, who founded Walmart. Think of the Mars family, which is behind the globally popular chocolate bar, as well as a number of other confectionery offerings. Then there is the Hermès family, which for six generations now has owned the French luxury fashion company famous for its Birkin handbags. The world's richest families own companies in industries as diverse as automotives (BMW), pharmaceuticals (Roche), hotels (Hyatt), supermarkets (ALDI) and cosmetics (Estée Lauder).

Of course, the wealth of these families is mind-blowing, often in the realm of tens (or even hundreds) of billions of dollars. It is also largely generational. In other words, the only reason these families are so rich today is because someone, at some time in the past, decided to change their personal financial future and create wealth for the generations that came after them.

The Waltons began by opening a single Walmart store at the tail end of World War II. Frank Mars began in 1902 selling molasses candies. Regardless of the product or the industry, what they did was show an entrepreneurial spirit that would ultimately create wealth for future generations.

While using these examples might seem outlandish, the point that I'm trying to make is that every one of these families had to start somewhere. When they took that first vital step, I doubt that they ever imagined their endeavours would continue to echo through generations of their family, but they did – and continue to do so.

## Money blueprint

Every parent wants their child to have a better life than they did, whether that means being better educated, wealthier or something else.

Fundamentally, building wealth means creating a blueprint. This is why wealthy people stay wealthy: when they have children, they instil the same principles that they have learned so their children can repeat the process of wealth accumulation. This is generational wealth in action. Today, these children are sometimes called 'privileged' – those whose parents are wealthier and have therefore created more opportunities and learnings for their children throughout their lives, including career advancement in specific industries.

In decades past, it was very difficult for most people to make the leap from lower to middle class, or from middle to upper class, because there wasn't the same access to wealth creation education that there is today. That meant that someone had to have an entrepreneurial mindset to change their own financial situation and start building potentially generational wealth.

Let's look at the vitally important first seven years of a child's life. During this period of time, children mostly learn from what they see as well as from the words that they hear from their parents.

A child who is growing up in a family that is struggling to make ends meet is likely to hear such things as 'money doesn't grow on trees' and 'we can't afford that'. Sometimes there may not even be enough money to pay for groceries every week. Living in this reality, where money is always in short supply, instils them with financial fears that they can carry through to their adult lives. Generally, this means that they will have a scarcity mindset rather an abundance mindset. Often, they will be fearful of doing anything that might impact their ability to keep a roof over their heads and put food on the table because of the experiences they had as a child.

However, a child who has been raised in an environment where money is not a problem will have had a very different experience. Perhaps their family talks about money or their family business at the dinner table, so children start to learn about finance and business from an early age. If their family already has some generational wealth, they may hear, 'If you work hard, you can do anything', or 'There's no point aiming for the middle'. Hearing such positivity around money means that this child has more chance of not only developing an abundance mindset but also learning smart money habits from their parents.

It's not difficult to predict which child is likely to have a more financially successful life, generally speaking, is it? And it's all because of what they saw and heard during those first seven years of life.

Many readers of this book probably experienced the first scenario but, because of more ready access to education, have been able to actively change their situations. It is no longer written in the stars that where you start off financially is where you have to end, as it used to be in decades gone by!

## Birds of a feather

According to Henry Ford, 'Failure is simply an opportunity to begin again, this time more intelligently'.

There are many wealthy people who have lost everything but learned from their mistakes and then tried again. In fact, many of them say that they were able to create wealth more quickly the second time around because of the lessons they learned when everything went pear-shaped the first time.

They have experienced failure and learned from it. Vitally, they were not afraid to try again. Basically, they have educated themselves and learned what works and what doesn't. This education and experience has given them the skills required to build wealth, and they can replicate the process time and time again.

In the early days, those early financial pioneers didn't have the benefit of reading books about the topic. Rather, they were often creating money-making principles as they went along.

Of course, it is completely different these days because there are many blogs, books, training programs and podcasts about creating wealth that anyone can access, usually with the touch of a button. In fact, it is probably easier than ever before for anyone to improve their financial education so they can retire younger and richer.

But there is still one factor that can up-end even the most educated of go-getters: friends and family. The people around you will make or break you through the habits and rituals that they have set, which you will probably end up following. So, the quickest way to become better in an area is to align yourself with the best in the field that you want to master.

There's a famous quote by Jim Rohn: 'You are the average of the five people you spend the most time with'. The energy they bring will become your thermostat. Just think of the friendship groups in your personal sphere – you will all generally have one interest in common. Even if they are people you have known since childhood, that is the shared experience that binds you together. In adulthood, there are friendship groups that revolve around sport, the arts and even partying! Birds of a feather flock together, after all.

If you hang around with five unfit people, you will probably wind up becoming the sixth unfit person. Conversely, if you spend time with five people who like to keep fit, perhaps by running, then over time you will become the sixth fit person because you will naturally adjust your fitness level to keep up with the herd. The same concept is true when it comes to creating your wealth blueprint so you can retire richer than the majority.

Now, I'm not suggesting that you decide to ghost any of your friends who don't have the same abundance mindset as you! Rather, I'm saying that you need to be more strategic about who you discuss your financial hopes and dreams with. If they don't have the same mindset and don't have a similar drive or inclination to improve their financial lot in life, they may be outwardly supportive of your motivation, but they won't be able to help you get there because they simply don't have the skills or desire to do so.

If you want to master money, it's best not to discuss it with any of your friends and family who don't have what you want or want it themselves. Instead, it's vital that you learn from the people who have the life that you want and are willing to share the secrets of their success with you. This is what I call 'hijacking', and I mean it in a very positive way. It involves learning from someone who has been there and done that so that you can fast-track your learning curve. The added bonus is that you can create the life that you want without having to experiment yourself – and pay the price of failures – because they have already done that for you and are happy to share their experiences with you.

Anyone with access to the internet can present themselves as an expert in anything these days, which is why it's imperative that you undertake your own research to determine whose model you want to follow. Fundamentally, though, anyone who is purporting to help you retire younger and richer must have actually achieved that themselves. Otherwise, their words are essentially without value.

Hopefully, it is clear to you by now that if there are people out there making their money work harder for them across a number of investment classes, there is no reason why you can't retire younger and richer, too. I am living proof of this, given that I started investing when I was an apprentice and today my wife Sophie and I have $10 million equity in a property portfolio valued at $20 million.

As I mentioned at the outset, I could retire today at just 32 and live a very good life, but that is not something I want to do.

That's because my goal now is to create a new generation of people who are committed to a better financial future than what their parents or grandparents achieved.

By heading to ypywmastery.com.au you will find more information on our courses, which teach our Mastery students how to build wealth the right way. At the time of writing we have had over 1200 students complete our courses.

In this next section, you'll learn how you can maximise your income so you can start investing in assets.

### Investment tip

Your mindset will become your financial beacon – what you think will become your reality. So, be careful about the company you keep, because subconsciously your mind will start to believe their words. Before you can transform your financial reality, you must transform your financial mindset. Once you subconsciously believe that you can build wealth, your mind will help you find a way to create it in real life over time. Now, don't be fooled; this doesn't happen overnight. This must become part of your identity, which is something you must practise so it becomes a habit for the rest of your life. Very similar to working out to improve your health and fitness, your financial mindset needs to exercised daily, too.

## Three income skills

No one has ever been able to create wealth without first having the ability to earn an active income. As I've mentioned, I bought my first property when I was earning apprentice wages, which are always low because apprentices receive on-the-job training and are learning new skills, so they are not as productive as fully qualified tradespeople. This just goes to show that even people on low wages can create the opportunity to invest if they are committed to achieving their goals.

I did have to scrimp and save to pull together the deposit, mind you. This book may teach you about the principles of retiring younger and richer, but hard graft is always needed to take that first vital step to creating wealth. There really is no other way around it.

Remember those super wealthy families I mentioned earlier? The reason why they are billionaires today – sometimes six generations after their ancestor 'did something' – is because they evolved the business and created multiple income streams over the decades. The Waltons added more Walmart stores; the Mars family added product offerings such as M&M's, Maltesers and Snickers. Adding more places to sell products, or more products to sell, supercharged their income streams, which they could then recycle into even more income-producing assets.

Over time, this creates passive income – regular cash flow that requires no additional effort or further expense to maintain. That is why these families are in the upper echelon of wealthy families today. The concept is the same for anyone who wants to create wealth, but you must master your income skills to get there.

I believe there are three skills necessary to create income, and you must master them to achieve the first principle of building generational wealth: sales, negotiation and management (see figure 1.1).

## Figure 1.1: The three income skills

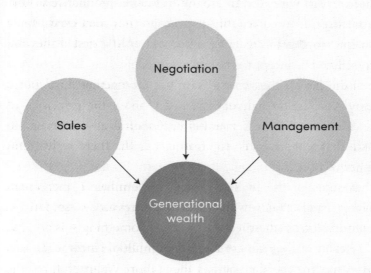

## 1. Sales

Sales is the most important income skill that you will need in your arsenal in order to achieve success – and when I say 'sales', I'm not talking about the ability to sell the aforementioned chocolate bars! No, what I'm referring to here is the ability to sell yourself to other people to increase your income over time.

The first requirement of this skill is to believe in yourself, because if you don't believe in yourself, how can you expect anyone else to believe in you? Once you have mastered the principles outlined in this book, you should have the self-confidence to sell yourself in the future.

Let's consider a couple of scenarios to illustrate what I am talking about here. It could be that you want to start a business but need funding to make it happen. This could mean you will need to sell your idea to a bank to secure the finance to turn your dream into a reality. Or perhaps your idea would be of interest to angel investors – again, you would need to be able to sell your concept to the types of people who can help your venture get off the ground. Without their support, your idea may never see the light of day.

The ability to sell, yourself included, is an important life skill that will advance your career and ultimately increase the amount of active income that you earn. It's not a coincidence that some of the highest-paying active-income jobs on the planet involve sales, which usually incorporate some form of commission payment.

Real estate agents are a great example of highly paid sales workers. The more properties they sell, the more they earn in commission. This means that their income is never capped and they always have the ability to earn more – as long as they also have the right systems in place. The very best sales agents generally make millions of dollars in commission each year. They have learned the art of multiplying their income – and they are usually reinvesting that income to help themselves make even more money.

Your ability to sell yourself will make or break your wealth creation efforts. Not only must you have a clear and precise understanding of what you want to achieve, you must be able to convey this to people who are usually very time poor. There is a reason why the term 'elevator pitch' exists, after all. Being able to crystallise your idea into a few short sentences, as if you literally only have a few moments with someone who can help improve your financial future, is essential. They don't want to hear your life story, or even the backstory of how you came up with the idea or the business that you want them to support. Rather, they want you to get to the point with confidence and with clarity.

The wealthiest people are always looking for opportunities to increase their incomes, not because they are greedy but because they have mastered the principle of building generational wealth, including creating multiple income streams that preferably have uncapped potential. They always have a team of expert advisers and trusty assistants as well, to whom they can delegate the task of early investigation into potential income-producing opportunities. Once the assistants have completed the due diligence, they will advise the investor of the potential of a particular new product or acquisition and whether it would be a good idea to add it to their portfolio of assets. They may then organise a meeting with the investor, because they recognise the value of their time and don't want to waste a single minute of it. The most successful families and individuals remain the key decision-makers in their businesses, but they also delegate down the line so that they can concentrate on more high-level thinking and outcomes.

### Investment tip

Successful selling comprises three parts:

1. **Knowing what you're selling.** Leave no doubt in the other party's mind that you know what you're talking about.
2. **Practising.** No one is born a salesperson; they learn to sell, often by doing a lot of it. So, if you don't think you're very good, you need to practise more and

learn that each rejection is getting you closer to the next 'yes'. You must keep your own emotions out of selling, because no one cares about you in the sales process, to be brutally honest. They only care about what you're selling and if it's something that they need.

3. **Believing in what you're selling.** If you believe to your core that what you're selling will benefit the other party, then you would be doing them a disservice not to try to sell it to them. This is where you gain the true confidence to sell successfully.

## 2. Negotiation

The second most important skill necessary to create income is your ability to negotiate. Some of the most successful and wealthiest people in the world are where they are today because they have superior negotiation skills.

Most of us don't realise that we negotiate in every part of our day-to-day lives. For example, we negotiate with our children when we want them to tidy their rooms, eat their dinner or go to bed at the allocated time. In our professional lives, some of us negotiate with clients to secure the best price for a product for our company, while most of us will have to negotiate with our bosses when we ask for a pay rise or even an extended holiday period.

Negotiation is the art of swaying a decision or outcome in your favour. Most people's experience with negotiation is quite limited because the majority of the products we buy and the services we engage come with a fixed fee. However, the best negotiators never take something at face value, even when they have been told that what they want to purchase – a new phone, for example – has a set price tag on it. Instead, they will ask the sales rep if that is the best price they can offer and whether they are throwing in any extras, such as headphones or a phone cover, as a sweetener with the deal.

Just remember that every person you meet who is trying to sell something to you probably has a set sales target they have to achieve every week or every month. This means that they have an incentive to leave room to move on price or extras if it secures them a sale and gets them closer to their target.

The same concept applies to creating wealth through the purchase of multiple income-producing assets. No one is going to offer the purchase price of a property straight off the bat (unless the price is well below market value and the vendor or sales agent doesn't know it). Rather, you negotiate on price to arrive at a figure, as well as terms and conditions, that are agreeable to both parties. If you can't do that then, clearly, no sale is made.

Negotiation plays a big part in building your pool of assets. You will be faced with negotiating time and time again over decades as you build up your portfolio. The better you are at it, the more money you can save and, ultimately, the more money you can make. As I always say, you make money on the way into a deal and not on the way out – contrary to popular belief.

Being aware of the market you're playing in can influence the way you negotiate. For example, in real estate you will have to assess the competition in the market you wish to buy in and also the frame of mind of the selling agent and vendor. If the market is cold and properties are taking a while to sell, you then have the upper hand to negotiate hard. Again, this all depends on where the price started, which is why it is vital to do your due diligence on the current market conditions beforehand.

For example, if a property was listed on the market for $700,000 and all similar properties in the area are selling for $750,000, then maybe your room to negotiate with that property owner isn't as large as it would have been if the property was on the market for $780,000. This doesn't mean that you didn't do a good job of negotiating the deal if you can't get the price lowered – in reality, you did a great job identifying the property as being under market value to begin with. Negotiation is all about getting a great deal and, never forget, that is the only outcome that you're after.

When it comes to negotiation, you're trying to find the weak points on the seller's side of the transaction. This can come down to understanding why someone is selling to begin with. Rather than ask outright why they are selling – that makes your intentions blatantly obvious – you need to ask questions around the situation. That way, you can draw your own informed conclusion about why they are selling without them having to say it directly.

Negotiations are all about leverage and gaining knowledge from a conversation to understand the situation to give you an advantage. This is why negotiation is an art – and the only way to perfect it is by doing a lot of it.

## 3. Management

The third and final income skill is management, which involves learning to manage and read people. To achieve financial success, whether in business or via investments, you must be able to manage people, their expectations and their favoured outcomes.

In the business world, the ability to understand the motivations of everyone involved in a deal can make or break the outcome. We've all had bad bosses in our lives who treat their staff as inferior, are bad communicators or have a closed-door policy instead of an open-door policy. The actions of these bad bosses prevent them from reading people effectively, which causes them to experience worse outcomes. You don't want to be a bad boss when it comes to your investment portfolio!

A key part of people management is the development of superior communication and listening skills. After all, there is nothing more frustrating than having a conversation with someone when you know they aren't really listening to anything you are saying, is there? Being an active listener will enable you to understand what the other party desires the most, which will enhance your chances of success at the negotiation table.

Using real estate as an example, it always surprises me when buyers get so fixated on the price of a property that they miss the opportunity to ask the sales agent what other terms and conditions might be equally important to the vendor. Yes, price is a big part of the negotiation, but there are usually other underlying terms and conditions that can sweeten a deal without any additional financial outlay. Perhaps the seller wants a longer settlement so they have time to purchase another property themselves, or they might desire a shorter settlement because they have already bought another property to call home. Another example is when the vendor might actually want to sell the property off-market because their privacy is the most important factor to them. These factors are all potential opportunities for buyers, but if you don't ask the questions, you will never know the answers.

If you want to retire younger and richer, the quickest way to increase your income is by learning how to manage people and complex situations. This will lead to your active income increasing, which will allow you to save more money and, in return, allow you to purchase more assets more quickly.

Over the years, I have learnt that the more money I make, the more balls I have to keep in the air at the same time. Managing doesn't stop with business or your job – it also extends to your life and assets. Most people never see the success they want because they have poor management skills and can't tolerate stress.

At the end of the day, the more you have, the more you manage, and therefore the more stress you will need to learn to cope with. Managing property managers, tradespeople and banks and finance is part and parcel of building your portfolio. The better you become at managing and delegating, the more time you can free up and, in return, the more money you can make.

*

By developing and practising these three income-producing skills, you will be on your way to changing your financial situation and potentially creating wealth that can be handed down through the generations of your family.

In most parts of the world, children are given the opportunity to be educated by attending primary and secondary school. Some people will go on to tertiary education, while others may start an apprenticeship, and some may begin their working lives straight from high school. However, too many people believe that the highest form of education is gained at college or university, when that is really where lifelong learning begins. The most important education you can receive, in my opinion, is an understanding of business and investments, which is often best taught through real-life successes and failures.

There are very few successful businesspeople out there who haven't made mistakes, but as Henry Ford said, they used the opportunity to try again 'more intelligently' so they became masters in the business world. They also mastered the skill of maximising and multiplying their income streams, which they then invested to compound the capital growth.

## Four wealth phases

If your goal is to create significant wealth that can be passed down to the next generation, there are four phases that you can complete over years or even decades (see figure 1.2).

Figure 1.2: The four wealth phases

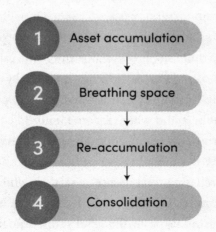

Whether you are investing in real estate, shares, businesses or cryptocurrencies, it is important to thoroughly understand the assets that you want to put your money into because your financial success will depend on how well these assets perform over long periods of time.

**HOT TIP** Never invest in an asset class you do not understand.

Your goal must always be to accumulate assets until you reach a point where the passive income from your assets is outperforming your active income on a yearly basis. This means that your passive income could pay for all of your living expenses so you no longer need to work and can retire younger and richer if you so desire. This is what I call the 'peak' or 'Holy Grail' of wealth creation, but to get there you need to follow – and complete – the following four wealth phases.

## 1. Asset accumulation

In the asset accumulation phase, you are channeling your active income (such as via wages or a salary) into acquiring assets. As your asset portfolio appreciates in value, you can then begin to leverage those assets to buy more assets by tapping into their equity. For example, if you buy a property for $600,000 using your savings and active income, and its value increases to $800,000, you now have $200,000 equity to 'leverage' to buy another property.

When purchasing real estate assets in this phase, your loan-to-value ratio (or LVR) will sit higher at around 80 to 90 per cent of the value of the asset. This means you borrow a far higher percentage of the purchase price to invest in the property compared to the deposit you have paid. It is important in this phase to have an emergency fund as a buffer. It's natural to have higher leverage at this stage, and it's smart to borrow to fund your investing. This will ensure you maximise the growth of your assets and shorten the timeframe to retirement.

### Investment tip

You need to think about debt in a whole new way. The more capital-growth-producing assets you buy and the more leverage you use, the more wealth you will create over time, and the more inflation will devalue that debt so you don't have to physically work to pay it off. The key is learning how to manage that debt – in the wrong hands, debt can be like a bomb, but it also can be one of the greatest wealth creation tools out there today.

Essentially, this phase is about going hard early on so that you can access compounding sooner by reinvesting profit into further assets to build your portfolio quicker. I believe being able to access leverage (or debt) is very important in the early stages of building wealth, which is why real estate assets are good here. Buying stocks in the accumulation phase makes it very hard to build your net worth quickly because you cannot leverage from one asset to the next or acquire debt multiples (the ratio of total debt to earnings before interest, taxes, depreciation and amortisation, or EBITDA) on your original investment.

Generally, when building your assets, diversifying into stocks and crypto should come during phase three, when you have access to more capital.

## 2. Breathing space

Once you have accumulated some assets, you need to wait for them to grow in value while also increasing your savings and your serviceability (lenders' assessment of your ability to take on more debt).

In the breathing space phase, you aim to increase your active income as well as your investment income (such as rent) while focusing on saving money. As your assets grow in value, your LVRs will naturally drop through capital growth, and your accumulation of savings will increase your financial buffer.

In this stage, you should look to uplift value in some of your existing portfolio through renovations. Then you can increase the rent and the value of the properties to get ready to access the equity for further purchasing.

Don't worry if you sit on the sidelines for a few years; this is normal and good for lowering the LVR of the portfolio so that you can get ready for the re-accumulation phase. In fact, I created my $20 million property portfolio over 13 years and only purchased assets in seven out of the 13 years as I moved through each one of the wealth phases. Always remember that nothing goes up in a straight line and these phases are all as important as each other to ensure you are building a safe and sustainable portfolio over the long term.

## 3. Re-accumulation

Once you have let your assets grow in value, increased your savings and improved your serviceability, you are ready for the third phase, which is to accumulate more assets in your portfolio.

During the previous stage, you lowered your LVRs on your portfolio, which has given you the equity to start purchasing more properties. Your emergency buffer should also be ready to support the second accumulation phase to build your portfolio safely. If you constructed a solid foundation of assets in the initial accumulation stage, you can now build off that strong support base.

You should have acquired enough safe assets and net worth to be able to diversify into other assets such as stocks and crypto if you so wish. This is when you can weigh up all of your assets and allocate a percentage of your net worth to each asset class. I like to allocate only what I am willing to lose to the riskier assets like crypto. This way I gain exposure to these newer asset classes without the risk of derailing my entire portfolio if something were to go wrong.

The thing to note is that if you're allocating only small amounts to crypto or stocks then the returns might not be worth the effort. For example, if you put $10,000 into crypto or stocks and it doubled to $20,000, and you then withdrew the funds, you would pay capital gains on half the gain (which is $5000) at your marginal rate of tax. So you might only end up with $8000 or so in your pocket, which isn't really going to change your life, and that investment is diverting your focus and energy away from more lifechanging moves. I chose strategically to invest in real estate for almost a decade before diversifying as I knew that was where I would build the majority of my wealth.

## 4. Consolidation

Consolidation is the process of shoring up your investments by improving your cash position and thus reducing your debt.

Once you have completed the re-accumulation phase and your portfolio has been built to a satisfactory level, you then consolidate by increasing cash buffers via savings in offset accounts and allowing your investments to increase in value once more. During this stage you can still look for more opportunities to increase your portfolio in the short term.

It is during the consolidation phase that you increase your rents so that you can focus on paying down your portfolio through the funds in your offset accounts.

The consolidation phase will be different for every person because how you proceed will depend entirely on your personal circumstances and wealth creation goals. That is, how soon do you want to live off the passive income and retire? You may hold the entire portfolio and pay down the debt for a period of time so that you maintain the portfolio's exposure to the market and to price increases, or you may want to sell some property early to access more of the income in the shorter term. There are no hard and fast rules during this phase because everyone's hopes and dreams are unique to them.

### Investment tip

A common strategy in real estate investment is the acquisition of burner properties. These are excess properties that you do not intend to keep over the long term but that will allow you to pay down debt in the consolidation phase.

Burner properties can be a useful part of your consolidation phase. While the term 'burner properties' might give the impression that they are throwaway assets, it is imperative that they still have the required investment fundamentals. Inferior properties have no place in portfolios designed to create wealth because they will never pull their weight in terms of capital growth or rental income.

Here is an example of how burner properties are used in a strategic property portfolio. Imagine you want to hold five properties unencumbered (with no debt) over a certain period of time so you can retire sooner and live off the rental income. To achieve that goal, you could purchase *eight* properties with the intention of selling three of them to pay out the debt on the remaining five holdings. This strategy works because those three properties will grow in value at a much faster rate than you can save your active income (or increase your rental income) to pay the down the debt on the other five holdings.

Say those additional three properties are valued at $2.5 million collectively and over 10 years they achieve an average growth rate of 6 to 7 per cent. You would have created an extra $2 million to $2.5 million in wealth over a decade. Of course, that is far more than the average person could ever save and far more than most people would even earn over that period time by trading their time for money!

*

I've mentioned already how it is beneficial to surround yourself with people who have the right mindset. The next chapter looks at money mindsets in more detail.

## Top 3 takeaways

1. To create generational wealth, someone must start the wealth creation process and, more importantly, teach their children along the way.

2. The most financially successful people surround themselves with others who have the same abundance mindset.

3. To retire younger and richer, you must master the three income skills of sales, negotiation and management, and work through the four wealth phases of asset accumulation, breathing space, re-accumulation and consolidation.

# Case study

## The next generation of financial success

There is no greater compliment than having someone entrust their child's financial success in you. That is exactly what Melbourne couple Joelle and Jason, both 49, decided to do after seeing their property wealth soar by $529,000 in less than three years.

They both work in the building industry but hadn't managed to acquire any real estate other than their own home, partly because they lacked the confidence to do so. However, in 2019 that state of play changed when they spent time in Brisbane working and also came across my podcast appearance with financial whizz Mark Bouris.

'When we were up there, we were going, "We should buy. Property is so cheap up here, what are we doing?" And then we still didn't have the confidence to take the next step,' Jason recalls. 'But when I listened to Daniel on the podcast and contacted him, the way he dealt with us was just great and we felt confident.'

It seems that their property-investment senses were more attuned than they realised, because once they decided to work with me, I recommended a house in one of the locations they had been considering – a seaside suburb in the Moreton Bay region.

'We felt comfortable that the investment was going to be the right decision. We still understood that it was our decision, but Daniel made us feel comfortable. He answered every question over and over again. He made himself available – even still now. Anything, any question, big or small, he's on the phone,' Joelle says.

That property was purchased for $450,000 in 2019 and experienced stellar capital growth of 60 per cent in three years, meaning Jason and Joelle realised $270,000 in equity from their very first investment property.

Within six months, with such spectacular results, the pair was keen to buy again because they had also started to understand how property investment could supercharge their financial future.

'You work so hard for your money, you don't want to lose it,' Jason says. 'But if you invest it this way then, all of a sudden, you're like, "That was a lot easier than working for the last ten years!"'

The second property was a house in Geelong that was purchased for $426,000 and saw capital growth of around 50 per cent ($214,000) in two-and-a-half years.

Before purchasing their third investment property using my expertise and experience, it became clear that their son, Mitchell, was also taking a very keen interest in their journey. The couple wanted to see their son start property investing much earlier than they had done.

'We wouldn't have encouraged Mitchell if we didn't feel comfortable. It had taken us years and we wish we would have done it sooner,' Joelle says. 'We're pretty excited that it's the one thing he listened to us about. He may not listen to us any other time but about that he did!'

Mitchell, now 24, works in traffic management and saved literally every penny he could to afford to buy his first-ever property, which was an investment rather than a home.

That house was in North Brisbane and was purchased for $350,000. After a cosmetic renovation – courtesy of the building prowess of his parents – the property soared in value by more than 65 per cent in a single year to be worth about $580,000 at the time of writing.

With results like that, it's fair to say that Mitchell was keen to go again. He recently added a second investment property to his burgeoning portfolio – all before he turned 25. His portfolio is currently valued at about $1.33 million.

Jason and Joelle also purchased a third investment property in 2022, which increased in value by nearly 7 per cent in just eight months. The couple's investment portfolio is now valued at $2.045 million with an impressive $529,000 in equity – all achieved within three years.

Feeling secure about their future financial position for the first time in their lives, Jason and Joelle decided to take their caravan for a six-month trip around Australia – something they had been wanting to do for a long time.

'We're grateful for Daniel because having the three houses set up the way they were gave us the opportunity to be able to take some time off while we're younger,' Joelle says.

And it appears that Mitchell has found himself a mentor, with the young man hoping one day to replicate my property investment success.

'Mitchell has said he wants to build an empire like Daniel. They are exactly his words,' Joelle says.

## Principle 2

# Create a money mindset

Remember that saying from the previous chapter that some of us used to hear from our parents when we wanted some spending money, perhaps to buy a new pair of sneakers or to go to the movies with friends: 'Money doesn't grow on trees'?

Of course, that statement is correct, but the truth of the matter is that money does grow somewhere, and that is in your mindset. The wealthiest people have not only created a money blueprint that they continually replicate, they have also developed an abundance mindset.

As T. Harv Eker once said:

'Whatever results you're getting, be they rich or poor, good or bad, positive or negative, always remember that your outer world is simply a reflection of your inner world. If things aren't going well in your outer life, it's because things aren't going well in your inner life. It's that simple.'

This quote fundamentally refers to creating the type of mindset where you see opportunity when others see roadblocks, and you are not prepared to settle for a future that is seemingly predetermined or 'in the stars' from the day that you were born.

## Why mindset matters

Your personal money mindset starts to be imprinted on you from the beginning of your life.

It's influenced by the financial situation of your parents and the parents of your friends at school. Depending on which school you attend, you may be surrounded by children whose families live week-to-week because they are perpetually trading their time for money in blue-collar jobs. Alternatively, your school (public or private) may be filled with the children of high-income professionals, which will have a different impact on money mindset.

For those of you who attend university, again, those around you may come from wealthy or privileged families, or they may not. Just think of how many parents in the USA squirrel away every dollar during their child's upbringing so that they may be able to help support them at a prestigious university, if they secure a hotly contested scholarship place at a blue-chip university such as Harvard or Stanford. (In countries such as Australia, students can attend any university they choose – including the top-ranked universities – as long as their academic performance is high enough for them to secure a spot.) And the reason why places in these universities are so sought after has as much to do with birds of a feather flocking together as it does with receiving an excellent tertiary education. A student at a top-tier university may well experience true wealth for the first time when they start hanging out with students from rich families, which will significantly alter the development of their own money mindset.

Now, I'm not saying that you need to attend or graduate from one of these universities to learn the skills to retire younger and richer. What I'm saying is that these types of environments – where an abundance mindset is the status quo – can make a huge difference to the financial success of its graduates because of the people they spend most of their time with while their brains are still developing.

The most financially successful families usually talk about money over the dinner table, too. They don't see it as a topic that should be avoided; rather, parents discuss their business dealings or their latest investments in front of their children, who soak up that information like sponges. That is why their money mindsets are usually more finely developed than children with working-class parents.

Money mindsets can be affected by movies as well, because the 'rich guy' is usually corrupt or has done something bad to make him so wealthy, hasn't he? These types of subliminal messages teach children (and adults) that money is essentially bad and the root of all evil! In reality, money is nothing more than the exchange of value that has been given to the open market.

> **HOT TIP** The more money received equals the more value given.

That's why, when it comes to building wealth, your relationship with money and how you perceive it is vitally important.

You see, you can never build wealth if you think that money is evil. That is like wanting to be fit but thinking that getting fit is evil, so you spend your time being jealous of fit people and never put in the time and effort to improve your overall health and fitness. All that being jealous of people who have done the very thing you want to achieve confuses your subconscious mind, because it is receiving the signal that the very thing that you supposedly desire the most is bad. It doesn't make sense, does it?

But there is a way to change this negative self-talk about money – and pretty much about anything that you want to achieve – and that is manifestation.

## The power of manifestation

Our minds use past experiences to inform our thought processes for future decisions. We always act based on what we have learned in the past. This is why some people who try to get ahead in life just never seem to make it, no matter how hard they try: their past learnings have taught them to react automatically to any situation with a scarcity mindset rather than an abundance mindset.

However, just because you didn't grow up in a wealthy family in which money was discussed regularly, or you didn't attend a school where the children of rich families were your friends, doesn't mean that you can't change your money mindset. And one of the most powerful ways to do so is via manifestation, or TEPAR.

Manifestation formula: $T \rightarrow E \rightarrow P \rightarrow A \rightarrow R$

Now, before you say, *Daniel, why are you teaching me algebra in this book?* these letters just represent an element of our money mindset that can be trained for financial success:

**T** = Thoughts

**E** = Emotion

**P** = Perception

**A** = Action

**R** = Results

Therefore, to put this manifestation into practice, it follows that your thoughts lead to your emotion, your emotion leads to your perception and your perception leads to action, which creates your results. It really can be as simple as that.

This manifestation formula can set you up for success and is something that I have personally been following for many years now.

Many people never master the formula in its entirety and often get stuck in the 'thoughts' and 'emotion' phases. Just consider someone with a scarcity mindset who might really want to improve their financial situation. They might think about trying to maximise their income by investing, but it's at that point that their emotions pipe up and loudly declare, 'Beware!' and their idea never makes the transition out of their heads to allow them to take the next vital steps.

However, people who have learned or created a money mindset have no problem transitioning their thoughts to actions and results because they have perfected and now follow a set formula – so much so that they don't really have any feelings about it at all.

I credit a lot of my success to the power of manifestation. Without question, it was fundamental in my early investing successes. But manifestation alone won't get the job done for you because at some point you do need to take action.

We all know of people who have big dreams of financial and investing success, who study property or share markets day in and day out, but who never actually do anything at all. There are myriad reasons why they may be stuck at this stage, with emotions being one of them and a lack of financial literacy being another.

What I love about manifestation is that you can practise it until you are blue in the face because it is free and available to each and every one of us. However, if you don't actually take the ideas out of your head and put them into practice, then they are just ideas and will never produce any tangible results – except perhaps disappointment.

The manifestation system I use involves a number of steps. First, I think about the desired income, net worth or personal goal that I want to achieve, and then I work backwards from there. Once I have the end goal, I need to map out every little detail about how I am going to create that wealth or achieve that goal, right down to the dollar, timeframes and how it will ideally unfold.

## The $10 million house... in my head

By mid-2022, I had created enough wealth that I could retire and live off about $300,000 per annum in cash flow from my various income-producing streams. However, that's not what my wife and I wanted to do. Rather, we wanted to help as many people as possible to achieve financial success so they can retire younger and richer, including via our popular Your Property Your Wealth Mastery Education courses (which you can access at ypywmastery.com.au).

I went to look at a $5 million property in Sydney that we wanted to be able to buy for cash at some point in the near-ish future. As I've mentioned, I've always used the manifestation formula to help me achieve my wealth creation and personal achievement goals, and I found myself doing that again on this occasion.

Once I returned home from that inspection, though, I realised that I didn't want to aim for a $5 million home – I wanted to aim for a $10 million home instead! But that big number didn't scare me, because I knew I could achieve it as long as I worked through the required steps to get there.

So, that same afternoon I sat down and visualised a $10 million house, and I started drafting the income and investment steps that were needed for me to get there. I knew that I needed to use the manifestation formula to devalue the number and alter my perception of the current reality, which was being able to actually afford a $10 million home at all. To be honest, I couldn't even afford a $5 million home.

By the end of that process, not only had I devalued the $5 million home and made it seem very easy, I had also made peace with that $10 million figure, because my brain had also begun connecting the dots to make it a reality.

It's crazy to see how the manifestation formula really works. In 2019, Sophie and I went to an open home, as we often did, to visualise our dream life. I turned up in my Jaguar car, as if I could afford the property we were about to see, but the reality was that I couldn't even afford the house in the backstreets.

We looked at this property near the water in Sydney that was on sale for $10 million. Sophie and I still have a photo of the day at that house and would always imagine living on this prized street. What a dream it would be for both of us!

Because I had worked through the manifestation formula and devalued the number to make sense of how I could achieve it, I wasn't intimidated by it; I just started working towards it straight away.

Fast-forward to 2023 and Sophie and I purchased a property on that exact street, right opposite that $10 million house, on the water. It was a special moment that I sat in for a long while and remembered a saying: 'What you can achieve in a year isn't very much, but what you can achieve in a decade is limitless'. It was a proud moment for both of us, for sure.

Fundamentally, this manifestation exercise enabled me to train my brain to achieve that goal, even though it seemed unrealistic at the beginning.

This example shows that if you want to achieve a specific goal, you must work out the steps you need to complete to help you achieve it. This is where I break my end goal down to bite-sized pieces so that I can start work on achieving them. This is a system that I implement with my business as well as my investments.

One of the biggest roadblocks when it comes to manifestation, as well as taking action, is becoming comfortable with the goals that you have actually set yourself, as I've just outlined.

My manifestation about the $10 million home enabled me to devalue and accept that figure so I was no longer emotionally triggered by it.

Some people might think their goals are too lofty and unachievable from the outset because of their underdeveloped money mindset, which means that they are unlikely to ever achieve them. When we set ourselves goals that are going to take a fair amount of time, dedication and discipline to achieve, there is always the chance that the goal just seems too big or too far in the future to ever achieve. That's why it's so important to create the pathways to follow to reach your financial destination.

## Manifestation in practice

When I was 16, I decided that one day I would own a Lamborghini. Most of my friends laughed at me, but what they didn't know was that I had manifested that I would buy a Lamborghini at some point in my life.

This dwarfed the goal to make it more achievable to me. Plus, having the goal of buying it 'one day' meant I would never be discouraged by a rigid timeline. I visualised it happening, and I created the stepping stones so that before I died I would indeed be the owner of one of the world's most luxurious cars. In early 2022, just 15 years later, I paid cash for a Lamborghini.

As well as manifestation, one of my stepping stones was to invest when I was young, rather than blowing my hard-earned cash as many of my friends were doing at the time. I lived as if I was broke for many years, because I knew this day would come – one day.

I even drove a $1500 bomb car (and blew it up twice) while living in a garage, just so I could save enough money to buy assets that would one day increase in value enough to allow me to do something as crazy as purchase my very own Lamborghini.

When I bought it, some people called me lucky, and others labelled me an 'overnight success'. But it was really all down to hard graft, dedication and working my arse off day and night, sometimes with little sleep, to achieve one of my lifelong dreams.

This is why I believe that anyone can do it – if they put their mind to it and dedicate themselves to learning how to build wealth and achieving their financial goals and dreams.

I liken building a money mindset to playing a video game: you don't automatically go to the end of the game and try to complete the last level, do you? You need to start with level one and then, once you've successfully completed it, you move on to level two, and so on and so forth.

This is the same with the game of life and investing! Even though you know your end goal and how you want to get there, you must start with level one. Along the way, you will complete levels that you thought weren't possible when you first started but now seem easy because of all of the skills you have learned and experiences you have gained along the way. This is what mastering your skills is all about.

Just think about those wealthy people I mentioned in the previous chapter who lost everything but were able to rebuild their wealth relatively quickly the next time around. Just because their business or investment venture didn't produce the results they were expecting, they didn't all of a sudden lose all of their knowledge about the process, did they? Instead, they brushed themselves off and did it all again, more intelligently this time.

One of the reasons manifestation is such a powerful tool for everyone is that it's free! Anyone can do it and practise it time and time again – mostly inside their own heads, but also by identifying and following the required steps to get to their end goal. Over time, you will build more self-confidence because of your evolving money mindset, which will enable you to believe that achieving your goal *is* possible.

You see, in my opinion, achieving something and manifesting it are virtually the same thing. Manifesting in such depth that your mind doesn't know whether it has already achieved the outcome or not ultimately breeds confidence.

For example, if you are currently earning $100,000 per year, but you really want to earn $1 million, the mere thought of supercharging your income ten times over would probably make your brain automatically tell you that you're a little bit crazy. You would be giving yourself excuses for why you can't do that, and the reality is that you probably couldn't at that stage. This is because you haven't learned the habits and skills required to multiply your income by that much.

But if you start manifesting earning $1 million a year, and you manifest that goal several times a day, every day of every week, something inside you will start to change.

Of course, you will need to understand in detail how you are going to actually achieve that $1 million annual income to allow yourself to believe that you can achieve it. Manifestation alone will never get you there, but it will start the process of training your brain to believe in the possibility. Through manifestation, you will have started wiring the belief in your brain that the end goal has already been completed. No longer will $1 million be a scary number, because you will believe to your core that you can achieve it. As I mentioned in my $10 million house story, it's all about dwarfing the number that seemed impossible so that it becomes not only a possibility but a certainty.

Back when I was earning $50,000 per year, I couldn't fathom earning $100,000 per year. But when I surpassed that income level and started earning $200,000 per year, I then looked at $100,000 as such a small number in comparison. By that stage, my brain told me this was just an earning capacity that I could attain because my skillset, experience and knowledge had surpassed that income level. The same is true for anyone who dreams of earning $1 million per year, or $5 million. You can achieve that income level if your mindset devalues and dwarfs that number, and you create and follow the steps to help you to get there.

## Playing to win

Top athletes are obviously naturally gifted at their chosen sports, but they are also big proponents of visualising winning. The same is true for wealthy people. Essentially, rich people play to win, and poor people play to *not lose*. How many times have you heard someone say, 'Don't invest in that business, real estate asset or stock because it's too risky and you might lose your money'?

This sort of mindset is held by people who are living in fear, often because of the money mindset that was instilled in them when they were children. These people will likely trade their time for money throughout their lives. They may have purchased their own home and even one investment property, and they have often made a little bit of money, but they have reached their maximum wealth creation level in their minds. Plus, they don't want to lose the money they have made, so they are constantly playing defence and not offence. They are not playing to win; they are playing to not lose what they have worked so hard to create.

Children from wealthier families tend to be more at ease doing 'big things' like investing because they have seen their parents (and probably their grandparents) do it successfully and they have been soaking it all up along the way. As I've mentioned, though, these days you don't need to have won the 'money gene lottery' to create enough wealth to retire younger and richer. You can do it by developing your money mindset and surrounding yourself with high-frequency people who lift you up rather than drag you down.

What makes a person 'high frequency'? The term can mean a lot of things, but I'm using it to refer to someone who conveys a sense of vitality, enthusiasm and active engagement with life or a specific aspect of life, in this case wealth creation. They are a high achiever who is always striving for success and continuously working to improve themselves and their circumstances.

Remember, your environment, including the people around you, shapes your thinking along with your achievements – birds of a feather flock together. In reality, this means that the longer you actively surround yourself with the types of people that you want to become, the clearer the steps to get there will become. High achievers generally spend time with other high achievers, after all.

This is why companies focus on their culture so much: they understand that one bad apple can spoil the bunch. They want to have a cohesive team of people who are positive and supportive of each other, not a team in which there are a couple of people who are always dragging everyone else down to their level.

Once you surround yourself with high-frequency people whose success you want to emulate – rather than those who don't have the same financial goals as you – you will start to see a noticeable difference in your mindset when you are with them versus when you are not. Why is that? It's because this state of high frequency is like a muscle that needs to be trained to reach its optimal state. It's a bit like when you first start going to the gym or working out with a personal trainer: for the first few weeks, your body is tired and sore as your muscles adapt to the new training regime, but after a while you likely won't have much muscle fatigue at all because your body is used to the program.

Similarly, when connecting with high-frequency people, at first your mind probably won't be able to operate at a high level for long periods because your broken belief system will unhelpfully chime in from time and time to try to revert your thinking to a scarcity viewpoint. Over time, though, that negative voice will become quieter and quieter because you are feeding your mind with abundant thinking and surrounding yourself with people who are playing to win and never to not lose. At some point, your money mindset will become similar to those high-frequency people, and you will become more like them than not. Your negative self-talk will disappear – and good riddance to it!

Remember, becoming the average of the five people you choose to spend the most time with – which can be physically or via networks or wealth-creation mentors – can help you reach their average income level. So please choose wisely, as you will organically match the frequency of these five people, which means you will either operate at higher frequency to achieve your goals or be dragged down to a lower frequency that may ruin your chances of ever achieving financial success.

Back in the introduction to this book, I talked about why most middle-class people would never become rich, which is mainly because they spend their entire lives trading their time for money. However, it is also because of the different money mindsets the two groups – the rich and everyone else – hold.

For example, if a wealthy person makes $500,000, they will automatically ask themselves how they can leverage that $500,000 to make more money. This is because they have an abundance mindset. Conversely, if a middle-class person makes $500,000 – say, in capital growth because of a market boom in their area – they will probably do nothing at all or even sell the property to take the money quickly. This is because they have a scarcity mindset.

Now, that $500,000 could easily be redirected into other income-producing and capital-growth-producing assets, which the wealthy person will definitely do without any emotion or hesitation. However, the middle-class person will probably not realise that profit until they sell their property at some point in the future. Indeed, they may never realise it in their own lifetimes if they decide to leave that property to their children after they die. You might think that means those children will then have a better start in life, but while it certainly will be better than nothing, they will likely be middle-aged by the time they receive the inheritance, and their learned money mindset will probably have prevented them from achieving significant wealth themselves by that time as well.

Hopefully by now you can see that creating a money mindset can make the difference between you retiring younger and richer or working until you are in your 60s or even 70s.

Likewise, please understand that your financial future is not set in stone from the day you are born anymore! We can all create wealth by ensuring that we associate with, and learn from, the people who are going to help us achieve our dreams, and not from those who don't share the same goals as we do and may even prevent us from achieving our goals at all.

## The five stages of your money success journey

There are five stages of building wealth that you must master to achieve money success (see figure 2.1). Each one of these stages is just as important as the others, and the stages should be completed in the order outlined here.

Figure 2.1: The five stages of your money success journey

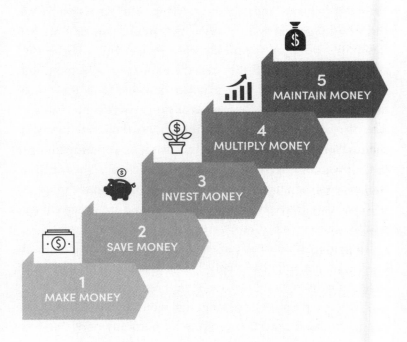

## 1. Make money

First, you must make money and learn how to increase the amount of money you make. This is vital. If you want to speed up the process of wealth creation, you need to make as much money as you can in the shortest period of time possible so you can then transfer that money into assets that will compound your wealth much faster.

By continually looking at ways to increase your income, you will increase your servicing capacity, which will allow you to borrow more money from the banks. More money equals more property and assets and, therefore, greater potential returns.

So, how can you increase your income? The number-one way to increase your income is to look first at the current skills that you have. These might have been acquired through your career or even through a weekend hobby. Then, take a look at your current job and ask how you can provide value to your workplace or industry.

Work out your true value and write it down. Then, set up a meeting with your boss and explain the value you bring to the company and the reasons you deserve a salary increase or bonus. Sometimes it is beneficial to negotiate a bonus with your boss if you do X, Y and Z to help the company hit a target. This removes the risk for the boss and makes it much more likely that you will get paid for the results you bring to the table. If you get the result, the company will grow, and you will get rewarded for it in return.

Another way to increase your income is to look at your current skills and work out how you can use them to create a side hustle.

**HOT TIP** It's much easier to make $10,000 than it is to save $10,000.

## 2. Save money

Second, you must learn how to save money. This is where most people get stuck. Making money and increasing your income is great, but if you don't save any of that income, then the increase will be for nothing.

Trust me, lifestyle inflation is a thing! Many people increase their income and then increase their spending to match, and so they never actually save any money whatsoever. This is a money habit that you need to keep in check.

The best way to keep your spending under control when you receive a pay rise is to set up a direct debit into a separate account to stop you spending that extra money. You will then be able to save your way to more deposits faster to enter the property market and grow your portfolio.

When I was younger, I had four different bank accounts:

1. **My 'everyday bills' account.** This was the account that all my income went into and all my bills came out of.

2. **My 'fun' account.** I would put a set amount into this account each week that I could spend guilt-free. If I didn't end up spending it that week, I would keep it there to save for a more expensive item that I wanted to purchase.

3. **My 'holiday' account.** I would put a set amount into this account each week that would go towards a break or getaway to recharge after having worked so hard.

4.  **My 'savings' account.** This was an account that I had with a different bank. It had no debit card so I couldn't easily spend the money. What can I say, I was young once upon a time and I knew how easy it could be to transfer money while out and about so that I could spend more. By having it in a different bank and with no card, I couldn't get the money transferred for a day or two, which stopped any irrational spending of my savings after a few too many beverages!

When I was younger and had fewer responsibilities, my rough rule of thumb for saving was 40 per cent. As I got older and had children and other bills to pay, it became 25 per cent. I would always monitor this percentage to see if I could increase the savings percentage without hurting my lifestyle. This was where the pay rises helped a lot!

> HOT TIP  Saving is a habit that needs to be instilled, like muscle memory. Once you have good saving habits, you're well on your way to creating more wealth.

## 3. Invest money

Investing your money sounds easy, right? Wrong. If it were easy, why doesn't everyone effectively invest all their money and retire within 15 years? When it comes to investing, the problem is that most of us are never taught how to invest, what to invest in or how it can allow us to retire younger and richer.

What we are taught at school allows us to fit into society and become worker bees. There is no formal education that teaches young people these five stages of the money journey, so how would they ever know how to invest correctly?

Investing your money is a vital step to getting out of the rat race. You can learn to earn money and save money, but if you don't invest it to make money while you sleep then it will be nearly impossible to retire early.

## 4. Multiply money

Multiplying money is powerful. Albert Einstein is credited with calling compound interest the eighth wonder of the world: 'He who understands it, earns it... he who doesn't... pays it'. That is one of the most powerful ideas in the world of finance summed up in a few words, and yet the everyday person doesn't truly understand compound interest or know how to apply it.

The people who take out liabilities (such as personal loans, credit cards and high-interest-rate loans) pay it, and they erode their chances of ever building wealth by doing so. On the other hand, those who learn about and understand compound interest use it to their advantage. They buy assets and let their value compound for generations. Ever heard of the saying 'the wealthy keep getting wealthier'? This is based on compound interest. The wealthy understand that if you acquire assets and hold them over a long period of time, the compound growth does all the heavy lifting.

So how do you multiply money? It's simple: you use a small amount of money as a down payment and then go to the banks to borrow the rest for an asset. Simply put, the quickest way to increase wealth is to use good debt.

If you buy an asset such as property, often you can borrow up to five times your initial deposit. So, instead of just getting a compounding return on your initial deposit, you get a compounding return on the deposit plus the debt that you used to purchase the asset.

I could keep going on about how this works but, put simply, if you can multiply your money by taking on good debt, allowing your assets to grow in value over time and then use phantom equity (which I discuss further in principle 4) to multiply your assets, you will be on your way to creating passive income. All of this is explained in much more depth in our Your Property Your Wealth Mastery Education courses (ypywmastery.com.au).

## 5. Maintain money

The fifth stage is the most important of all: you must learn to maintain your newfound wealth or the whole process will have been for naught.

A 20-year study on families that had created generational wealth made the interesting finding that nine out of ten families lost their wealth by the third generation. The simple fact is that the money principles and habits that were used to create the generational wealth were lost throughout the generations. So, even though you might learn and master the first four stages of building wealth, that doesn't mean you will know how to keep that wealth!

Keeping it comes down to understanding how to manage large sums of money and assets for long periods of time, often longer than you're alive. You need to teach these principles to your children so that they can maintain the wealth beyond your lifetime.

## Top 3 takeaways

1. Your money mindset starts developing from childhood as you learn from the money actions (and reactions) of your parents. If there is never enough money to go around, children will develop a scarcity mindset, but children from wealthier families will develop an abundance mindset.

2. The power of manifestation is that it can train your brain to devalue big-number goals. This means that you can make peace with achieving a figure rather than being unsure about whether you can achieve the figure at all. Manifestation only gets you so far, though, because you must also create and follow the required steps to achieve your goal at some point in your life.

3. Successful sports stars are obviously naturally gifted at their chosen endeavours, but they are also big proponents of visualising winning. The same goes for creating a money mindset, because wealthy people always play to win, whereas poorer people play to not lose.

# Case study

## Business and investment acumen from a young age

Five years ago, with adventure on his mind, Sydneysider Gordon packed up his bags and headed overseas. He had started his fire emergency plan design company a few years before, which he could manage from anywhere in the world – so he did.

In 2011, as a 24-year-old electrician, he bought his first property, which was a run-down unit in Sydney's Sutherland Shire. His desire to own property while still in his early 20s was partly due to the financial lessons he had learned from his parents.

'I wanted to move out of home, and I'd always been taught that if you didn't own anything and you were paying rent, it felt like dead money,' Gordon recalls. 'I didn't want to pay someone else's mortgage, so I looked at what I could afford at the time. It had peach-coloured cabinetry, and all the door handles were falling off and needed a bit of work. It was good, I saw potential, and because of that I got it at a better price.'

Fast-forward to March 2020, when Gordon arrived back in Australia to live just before COVID-19 forced us all into lockdowns. The timing was perfect, as it turned out, but completely accidental given he was simply returning home to work on his business and hopefully settle down. Given the uptick in safety requirements caused by the lockdowns, his business boomed during the pandemic, and his staff increased to nine.

By early 2021, Gordon had started following me on Instagram and admits he watched my commentary and market analysis for many months before contacting me. At the time, Gordon was keen on buying an investment property in Brisbane, a market that he knew I was active in as well.

'I liked Brisbane as an investment location because there were definitely a lot of universities and major infrastructure projects, and people were moving from New South Wales and Victoria up to Queensland in droves, so it seemed like a hot market to me,' he says. 'But I knew I needed a buyer's agent because I didn't have enough local market knowledge or the time to do it myself, so I reached out to Daniel and the rest is history.'

By March 2021, I had helped Gordon purchase a house with splitter potential in northern Brisbane for $470,000, which increased in value by 45 per cent in just 20 months. Gordon was so happy with the result that, with his business booming as well, he was ready to go again within a few short months.

'All of a sudden, the business was growing, and I did have that expendable income to look to invest,' he says. 'I do want to grow quite a large portfolio of a combination of property and shares, and I was in a position to be lucky enough to fire pretty soon after. As quickly as my mortgage broker could get it sorted was as quickly as I was ready to go again.'

That second property was a house in the eastern suburbs of Brisbane that was purchased for $600,000 and grew in value by 30 per cent in just a year. Both properties have seen solid increases in their weekly rents as well.

Gordon went on to purchase another house in Perth in 2022 and admits he used a different buyer's agent only because I wasn't yet purchasing in that location, but he says the experience was quite lacklustre.

Today, Gordon is travelling around Australia with his partner while also running his business from his caravan. He is the proud owner of a $2.5 million property portfolio at the age of 35. But he's only getting started, he says, with plans for more property purchases and an early retirement in the years ahead.

'I'd like to buy four or five properties in the next two to three years, as well as a commercial premises for my business,' he says. 'In ten years' time, I hope to be working minimal hours or not at all.'

And, given his continued wanderlust, it's safe to say he might be on a sailboat with a fishing rod in hand then, too.

Principle 3

# Master consistency and maximise your time

We've all seen overnight success stories, haven't we? Perhaps it is a newly famous singer or band, or it could be a new tech invention that suddenly makes its developer a billionaire when it is listed on the stock market.

Notwithstanding some rare examples where a person became rich beyond their wildest dreams from their first ever idea, the vast majority of ultra-successful people have worked hard for many years to perfect their craft before their endeavours start to produce any tangible rewards at all – financial or otherwise.

So, 'overnight successes' are generally the result of at least ten years of hard graft that nobody has seen or is overly interested in, either.

Think about the fact that Warren Buffett, who is generally considered to be the smartest investor in recent history, didn't make his first billion dollars until he was 60 years of age (although he did make his first million when he was in his early

30s, which was a goal he set himself when he was just 13). Now, more than 30 years later, his net worth is about $115 billion.

It took him two-thirds of his life to create that first billion dollars, but all of the lessons he learned along the way enabled him to multiply it 115 times over in half of the time that it took for him to reach that first financial milestone!

Over the decades, Buffett – as well as most financially successful people – have mastered consistency and maximised the value of their time to increase their wealth.

Of course, I'm not in the same league as Buffett by a very, very long stretch, but I started learning everything I could about investing when I was just 16 years old. I kept educating myself and saving nearly every penny I made to invest. By the time I was 26 – a decade later – I was a millionaire. Fast-forward six more years – so, half the time that it took for me to create that first million dollars – and I have turned that $1 million into $10 million worth of equity, cryptocurrency and cash.

One of the main reasons I was able to achieve this was my ability to create habits and rituals for success long before that success actually happened – and you can, too.

## Success habits

In some societies, many people find it difficult to understand why wealthy people are wealthy. They see the outcome but not the daily habits and consistency that those people have put in place that become the rules they live by each and every day, allowing them to win the day and continue to work towards their goals.

It stands to reason that anyone who wants to retire younger and richer needs to imitate the habits of those people who have already achieved this so they, too, can achieve financial success. Fundamentally, this means that you need to create the habits that are congruent with the outcome you're seeking. We can all say when we are 13 (like Buffett) or 16 (like me) that we want to be millionaires, but just saying it out loud will never make it happen.

As I mentioned in the previous chapter, you must follow this up with action or you will never achieve your goals. Many people say their dream is to have a big house or a nice car, but their actions and habits don't reflect the life that they're actually seeking to achieve. Instead, their dream remains just that – a dream that they never really did anything about achieving at all. The most successful people, on the other hand, set the goals that they want to reach and consistently work towards achieving them step by step.

Say, for example, that you have a dream to be fit and healthy, and perhaps even to have some impressive abs. How do you think you are going to achieve that physique? By diligently going to the gym and perhaps working with an expert such as a personal trainer who can help you to achieve your goals? Or by sitting at home on the sofa watching fitness influencers on an app while eating junk food?

No matter the goal, whether it is rock-hard abs or having $1 million in the bank, the reality is that if you are not creating daily habits that you consistently follow then you will never get there. Consistency comes from the completion of daily habits or routines that you follow so religiously they eventually become automatic.

**HOT TIP** Habits are the actions that create the outcome.

No matter what result you are seeking, your ability to achieve it will fundamentally be determined by your daily habits. Of course, there are good and bad habits in every aspect of life, such as eating well and regular exercise, or having a bad diet and not moving your body enough at all. When it comes to mastering your wealth, you had better master your habits first to ever stand a chance of succeeding.

### Investment tip

One of the very early habits that I developed was the ability to save. I made sure that I saved a large portion of my income – at first this was around 40 per cent because I lived at home with my parents – and I would put the savings into a bank account with no debit card so I couldn't access the money easily. This forced me to save it. If I felt like spending it, it would take around two days (back then) to transfer it to an account I could access with a debit card so I could spend it. Those two days gave me time to think about whether or not I really wanted to spend my hard-earned savings on something probably frivolous.

I always made sure that I was saving for a purpose, which made it harder to spend willy-nilly. I also liked to have certain rules around money. One of those rules was to never spend more than 10 per cent of my net worth (assets minus debts) on liabilities such as loans for cars, boats or caravans. This allowed me to reward myself as I increased my wealth over time without feeling guilty because I never broke my rules.

## Persistence pays off

When it comes to my own personal financial success, I believe it is my ability to be persistent and consistent that has enabled me to create an eight-figure asset portfolio by my early 30s. I actually believe that persistence is one of my superpowers because no matter what challenges have been thrown at me, I have always persisted until I achieved the outcomes that I had set for myself. Sometimes I was stubborn and unapologetic about where I wanted to go in life and how I was going to get there, no matter what obstacles lay ahead of me.

## Not taking no for an answer

When I was around 27, I had created a $4 million property portfolio, and at the time my mortgage broker told me to be happy I got this far and that I wouldn't be able to go any further because servicing my loans would be an issue.

Confused, I asked him, 'So, what do I need to do to keep moving forward?' He said I needed to increase my income and pay off debt.

So I spent the next two years paying down debt and increasing my income. I remember around 18 months later I wanted to purchase my own home for around $1.6 million. It was right when COVID-19 hit and I thought I could buy this house for way less than it was actually worth. I asked my broker, and he told me that I couldn't purchase the property and that my income wasn't enough because of my existing portfolio, which was not the news I wanted to hear.

So I started looking for another broker to see if they could help me, but by the time I found another finance broker the property had sold. The funny thing is that the new broker told me he could get me the money, but by then it was too late.

Fast-forward two years and that property has now increased in value from $1.6 million to around $3.5 million. What a way to lose almost $2 million, huh?

But through persistence I found myself a new broker who helped me take my portfolio from $4 million to over $15 million in three years. The reason I was able to break through to the next level of the wealth game was because I was persistent in finding out how to get there and dedicated enough to stick with it even though I knew I was going to have to work towards it for a couple of years.

As I wrote about in the introduction to this book, I am from a blue-collar or working-class family. My parents have an entrepreneurial spirit, though, which means that they set up their own business and invested whatever extra money they had into real estate assets.

As I was growing up, I not only started to learn about investing from them, but I also witnessed them forever trading their time for money, which is the second part of this principle and which I will discuss shortly.

However, because of where we lived and the schools that I attended, my dreams of financial freedom were not common among my peers, who mostly seemed to have made peace with their lot in life and with the fact that they would probably spend their lives working for someone else. Hopefully they would earn enough to buy a home for their family, and then one day they would retire and survive on the pension or their meagre savings for a decade or two before their time on this earth was done.

As you will know by now, that sort of life and that kind of retirement never appealed to me. But my dreams were so large back then that most people around me just couldn't fathom the possibility that a kid who didn't come from a wealthy background could ever achieve massive financial success. I definitely had more naysayers than supporters in those days.

In fact, if there is one thing that I learned from my experience back then, it is to be careful who you share your wealth creation dreams with. Most of my friendship group when I was younger didn't have the same financial dreams as I did, especially when I was working as an apprentice and then a freight train driver.

As I mentioned in principle 1, it's vital that you surround yourself with people who not only share the same goals as you but who are also going to champion your dreams, not try to destroy them just because they are not the same as theirs. This means that if you know where you want to head in life, and you have a clear path and understanding of how you are going to get there, make sure the people you share your dreams with can also see your vision and will encourage – and not distract – you along your journey.

I've used the phrase 'birds of a feather flock together' already in this book, but it's worth mentioning again because it's a crucial concept for anyone who wants to achieve more than their school chums, their circle of friends or even their families ever have. The most successful people are discerning about who they spend their valuable time with, and they are even more careful when it comes to the people they choose to learn from or work with.

Many people with big dreams simply hang out with the wrong crowd. Now, I'm not saying that you should stop spending time with your friends and family! What I mean is that if you want to retire younger and richer, and you want to learn about creating wealth, then there is no point in sharing these aspirations with people who don't have the same goals or dreams as you. By surrounding yourself with like-minded people, you give yourself the best opportunity to reach your goals by learning from people who have been there and done that – and who are happy to share the secrets of their success with you.

Head to ypywmastery.com.au to find more information on our Mastery courses, where you can meet like-minded investors on the road to retiring younger and richer.

## How to maximise your time

The second part of this third wealth creation principle is one of the most important parts of this book, in my opinion. That's because if you spend most of your life trading your time for money via wages or a salary, you are rarely going to have enough energy or motivation to create opportunities to increase your net worth.

One of the most obvious differences between wealthy people and average income earners is that wealthy people value their time more than anything else. And I'm not talking about work-life balance here; I mean they are focused on freeing up their own time wherever possible so that they have the clarity to consider what their next move is going to be.

When I was a low-paid apprentice, my job required about 80 per cent of my usable time and energy every week. I worked six days a week, and by Sunday I was so physically and mentally drained that I had no energy to do anything but spend time relaxing with my friends. But because I had already started educating myself on wealth principles, I also recognised that if I continued on this path, I was never going to get anywhere in life because I would always be too tired to do much more than work every day for someone else, which I didn't want to do – even though at the time that someone was my dad!

One of the reasons why most people spend a lot of time talking about investing but never actually do anything is because they are not prepared to put in the time and effort from the outset to make their dreams a reality. When you are starting out on your journey to improve your financial lot in life, there really is no way around the fact that you may have to burn the midnight oil to start the process. No one can just quit their job so they can solely focus on changing their financial future, especially because you need to be earning an income if you are borrowing funds to invest in an income-producing asset.

While there is a variety of experts who can assist you these days, the onus still needs to be on you to manifest your goals, create an action plan and then put in the hours to put your plan into practice. This means you have to be willing to work all day at your job – trading your time for money – and then spend whatever time you have available at night to work on your dreams. For some people, this may be after the children have been put to bed.

Essentially, you must adopt a 'whatever it takes' mentality if you truly want to create financial success. You must be passionate about your goals and relentless in your pursuit of wealth. There are no short-cuts here. You must understand your 'why'.

## How cancer motivated my 'why'

As I've touched on in the early chapters of this book, one of the defining moments in my life was when my mum was diagnosed with breast cancer. She was only 40 at the time, so the diagnosis was a massive shock to everyone in my family. I was only 19 and was working for my dad as an auto electrician. The cancer was already at stage three by the time it was picked up by doctors and Mum's chances of survival were very low.

I vividly remember the sense of panic that radiated through-out my family at that time. As a teenager, you never contemplate the death of your parents, do you? But that became a reality to me in the space of a few short hours. I can honestly say I was never the same person again.

It was during my mum's cancer fight that my 'why' about building wealth was crystallised. I knew that I wanted to do anything I could to ensure that my parents would have everything they ever needed in life.

As I mentioned previously, my parents were small business owners, and anyone who has ever worked for themselves knows there is no sick or holiday pay (although these days it is always advisable to have some sort of income protection insurance for situations such as these).

Mum and Dad had worked hard all their lives and invested in real estate with any additional funds they had available, but as soon as Mum was diagnosed they were at risk of losing everything they had. Of course, Dad wanted to be with Mum throughout her cancer battle, so he virtually quit the business immediately – leaving me, a young apprentice, to manage it as best I could. I think I did alright because we managed to keep the doors open throughout Mum's ordeal. But as a family, we still needed money to survive during those trying times, so my parents sold some real estate assets to create much-needed cash flow for the household.

I vividly remember the additional emotional stress of Mum's fight to stay alive amid a constant battle to find enough money to survive financially.

At the same time, I was going into work every day and trying my hardest to keep the business afloat, when I had an epiphany of sorts. It suddenly occurred to me how important money is during times of crisis. If my parents hadn't had that property to sell, we would have lost everything, so we were probably better off than many other working- or middle-class people might have been in the same situation.

Many successful people have experienced trauma of one kind or another when they were young and used it as motivation to transform their lives for the better. It was the same with me. My mum's cancer battle and our fight to have enough money to keep our family afloat created a burning desire in me to never let that happen to anyone I loved ever again. This is exactly when my 'why' was created.

Even though her chances were so slim, my mum is a proud breast cancer survivor these days, and I have achieved the goals that I set myself back then many times over.

You don't need to have such a significant moment to understand your 'why', but knowing yours is a vital part of the wealth creation process. Perhaps it could be that you want to retire at 35, buy a boat and sail around the world. Or, it could be that you want to create generational wealth for your family.

Your 'why' is personal to you and can be whatever you choose, but unless you know what it is you will struggle to achieve your goals, because you don't actually know where you are heading, do you?

### Investment tip

Your 'why' will be your strongest motivation to achieve the success you seek. Becoming successful can sometimes take decades, and it is the 'why' that you draw upon when you're down and out and ready to quit. Let your 'why' be the compass you follow during your journey.

## Time value

As I mentioned at the start of this section on maximising your time, the wealthiest people value their time more than almost anything else. They understand that if they waste their time on endeavours that will not maximise their wealth creation efforts, then they are not using their time optimally.

Fundamentally, wealthy people compound their net worth by actively freeing up more and more of their time so that they can multiply their income. One of the ways that they do this is by leveraging other people who can assist with duties or tasks that are not going to improve their financial position.

I know it's a bit of a joke in society, but 'rich' people always seem to have cleaners, don't they? For outsiders looking in, the fact that they don't even have to clean their own homes appears to be one of the many benefits of being wealthy.

The reality of the situation is that anyone who values their time and earns more than a domestic cleaner should employ a cleaner, in my opinion. Rather than spending five hours a week cleaning your home, you could pay someone to do it for a fraction of the cost of the time that you would have lost doing it yourself. Consider a professional couple who earn $200,000 per year, which is about $100 per hour. Domestic cleaners make about a third of that (depending on your location). Simple maths shows that paying a cleaner for two hours a week costs that professional couple about $60, versus $200 of their time if they were to do it themselves. In fact, two hours of professional cleaning could be the equivalent of five hours of cleaning that you do yourself, which means you're saving even more time and money.

Think of it this way: if you work the standard five days a week, and at night you spend time with your family and children, then there is very little time left over for you come up with ideas to create wealth, start businesses or invest the money you have earned, is there? The wealthy understand that in order to progress, they must keep freeing up their time to move on to bigger and better things.

Obviously, there are limits to how much of your time you can free up in the beginning, because you will likely have a finite amount of spare cash that you can pay someone like a cleaner or a gardener. However, by understanding the principle of maximising your time to focus on your investing endeavours, you can incorporate some of these options into your own household budget.

There are only 24 hours available to each of us each day, but some people pack so much into those hours that they are classified as 'high achievers'. The reason they are seen this way is because most people can't fathom how they can achieve so much in a single day when they struggle to get through the daily grind themselves. One of the reasons for their high achievement is these people have an abundance mindset. They also value every single second of every single minute of every single hour of every single day. Indeed, they are true proponents of the saying 'there is no time to waste'. Over the years, I have taken this mindset to heart and practise this principle without question every single day.

## My daily routine

- **6 a.m.** After I wake up, I usually get changed and go straight to the local pool to swim some laps.
- **7 a.m.** I have breakfast and a shower.
- **8 a.m.** I take my dogs for a walk with my wife and children, and we talk about the business, personal goals and plans. We usually reflect on the things we are grateful for in life together.
- **9 a.m.** I get into my (home) office and call my team to see how things are going with the business. This is when I delegate jobs for the day as well.

- **9.15 a.m. to 11.30 a.m.** I start my client meetings and usually work until lunch, when I break for around one hour – this used to be around 20 minutes when I was building the business.

- **12.30 p.m. to 6 p.m.** After lunch, I work until 6 p.m. before calling it a day and spending some time with the family or working out in my home gym. I usually work on some content creation for my social media following during the night as well.

Throughout each workday, my meetings with clients are non-negotiables in my diary, but I delegate other projects that I am working on, such as podcasts or video editing, and renovations or developments. I try to leverage as many people as I can to get through more in a week than most people would in three months.

I am also always working towards set goals each day, which I measure after each time period. My goals are generally allocated into the following periods:

- **12-month goals.** These can be KPIs in business or even in my personal life around where I want be mentally, physically and financially.

- **Six-month goals.** These are my yearly goals broken down into two parts so they are more manageable. You don't want to work on all your goals at once; instead, prioritise a few goals at a time.

- **Quarterly goals.** Usually I am working on three to four different goals that are being measured within a quarter. Some goals are smaller and I will complete them in a quarter, while others will continue over the entire year. The idea of this is to show yourself that you're progressing.

- **Monthly goals.** This is where your large goals are broken down into bite-sized tasks.
- **Weekly goals.** These are very small parts of a larger project. Very much like building a house, here you're not focusing on the house but on the next brick that needs to be laid.

Each week I determine my priorities so that I am always progressing towards the bigger picture. I measure my progress and make sure I am on track to hit all the goals I have set myself for the year.

I also always reflect on my week and take a look at what I have personally dedicated my time to, and then for each task I ask myself, 'Can this be done by someone else so that I can achieve more?'

**HOT TIP** Goals that are measurable, with a timeframe for completion, get done.

## Top 3 takeaways

1. Most successful people have spent years learning and perfecting their areas of speciality, including developing positive habits that they repeat so consistently they become automatic.

2. Once you have developed your goals and understand your dreams, you must remain committed to them and persistently work towards achieving them, no matter what life might throw at you.

3. The wealthiest people value their time more than almost anything else because they understand that unless they have the time and space to think, they won't be able to make meaningful progress towards their goals.

# Case study

## Making the most of the market and your own abilities

When Richard was 18 and a builder's apprentice, his father suggested he buy a property in Tasmania to start his property journey. This seemed like a good idea to Richard as it would force him to save some money.

Little did he know at the time that over the next 15 years he would go on to buy and sell four properties, realising a reasonable profit and trading up each time to something better, often courtesy of his building prowess.

Richard sometimes laments that he really shouldn't have sold those other properties over the years. 'I knew nothing about property investing back then,' he recalls now.

Today he lives on the South Coast of New South Wales with his schoolteacher wife, Rebecca, and their three children, in a home he built for their family. But a few years ago, Richard and Rebecca, who are in their early 40s, realised that they needed to do more to improve their financial future, especially given Richard is self-employed and has minimal superannuation.

At the start of 2020, Richard's brother suggested he listen to an episode of my podcast as I sounded very similar to him – that is, someone who invested as a young man on apprentice wages. Also, he recalls, the episode featured a case study that spoke about the exact situation he was in – nearly owning your principal place of residence with lots of equity that you're not using, and also having very little super or not enough money for retirement.

Richard had previously reached out to other buyer's agents and had inexperienced people talk to him, so he was not willing to spend his time or money with them. So, after listening to the podcast episode, he called Your Property Your Wealth and I answered the phone, which impressed Richard given he had reached out to other high-profile buyer's agents and never even heard back.

By this stage, most of the country was in lockdown and many commentators were predicting property price falls. However, the smartest investors and buying experts recognised that an almighty boom was on the horizon.

When I recommended that the couple purchase a house in the eastern suburbs of Brisbane, Richard was admittedly nervous, but the level of research and data analysis I presented to him encouraged him to push ahead. That three-bedroom house settled in June 2020 and was purchased for just $440,000. By the end of 2022, it had increased in value by an extraordinary 59 per cent.

A few months after buying that house, now much more confident, Richard and Rebecca decided that they were ready to purchase another house, this time in the northern suburbs of Brisbane.

'I just knew I had to keep going. I knew I wasn't going to stop at one, so I thought, there's no time that's better,' Richard says.

That property had a long-term lease with Defence Housing Australia, which gave the couple security of tenancy during the lumpy rental days of 2020. The couple paid $445,000 for that property, and within two years it had increased in value by an impressive 55 per cent.

Richard also says that something happened between the purchase of the first and second properties that made him understand the superior property selection fundamentals I abide by.

'We pulled out of two other properties which we were bidding for because both of them had bows in the ceilings,' he recalls. 'One of the many things that gave me a lot of confidence was the first time it happened, instead of Daniel just pushing the sale forward, he said, "No, we're out. Let's just walk away". Then it happened again, and he said, "We're out. We'll find something else," even though he knew it was hard to buy at the time.'

Six months later, in April 2021, the couple was ready to go again, and this time I helped them secure a house in Geelong, just outside of Melbourne. Richard was keen for the couple to diversify their portfolio, and he liked the fact that I also owned properties in Geelong. That property was purchased for $482,000 and by the end of 2022 (18 months later) it had produced nearly 29 per cent capital growth.

After a good couple of income years, Richard knew he wanted to add one more property to the couple's growing portfolio, so in October of 2021 I helped them secure a house in northern Brisbane with a still-affordable purchase price of $505,000. That property grew in value by nearly 25 per cent in the first year.

In the space of just two-and-a-half years, Richard and Rebecca saw their investment property wealth soar by more than $750,000, which he admits they are so over the moon about that they have recommended my services to friends and family members.

'I can't believe that it's turned out this well. It couldn't have been much better, really.'

## Principle 4

# Make leverage your superpower

The term 'leverage' gets bandied about in financial circles a bit like confetti, and there's a reason for that: leverage is the superpower of highly successful people.

Leverage can be defined as an investment strategy that uses borrowed money to increase the potential return of an investment. When people succeed in growing their wealth, often it comes down to their understanding of leverage and their ability to rationalise and accept using borrowed funds to increase their own wealth position.

The vast majority of investors will only purchase one (or maybe two) investment properties, often because they don't want to take on too much debt. What they fail to understand is that mortgage debt is good debt, because it is used to buy an income-producing and capital-growth-producing asset that will help them to retire younger and richer.

Fundamentally, leverage comes in many forms. Wealthy people understand that leverage can be extremely powerful because it can help give them back time, as per my insights in the previous chapter, but also it assists with return on investment and knowledge.

Likewise, the wealthy understand the concept of 'phantom equity'. Equity is the difference between the amount of the loan you took out to purchase an asset and the current value of an asset. You can extract that equity – minus a percentage retained as a buffer – to invest in another property, which then builds equity as well. I like to refer to this as phantom equity. The equity from the first property was built on an initial investment that you had to work for, but you never had to work for the money that phantom equity is built on. Phantom equity is powerful because it's like real-life money growing on trees: you plant a seed and, once it grows, you use the offcuts to grow even more!

However, there are different types of leverage that you can use to supercharge your wealth creation efforts, with return on investment being one of the most important.

### Investment tip

Leverage is the key to wealthy people's success and is used in business as well as investing in assets. You can use leverage either to save time or to multiply profits.

## Return on investment

As I mentioned in the previous chapter, the wealthy use the skills of other people to buy back more of their own time. They then leverage their earned income into assets that will create passive income for them over time.

One of the simplest ways that they create passive income through leverage is by leveraging their savings to secure a loan so they can buy assets that will increase their cash flow as well as their wealth position.

> **HOT TIP** Return on investment is a percentage calculated by dividing the profit earned from an investment by its cost and multiplying by 100.

What's important to understand is that regardless of the fact that you are using borrowed capital to purchase assets, your return will always be based on the total value of the holdings that you have acquired.

## Leverage in action

Let's say that you have $500,000 and are ready to invest. If you kept it in the bank, you might return interest of, say, 2 to 5 per cent in a good year, or $10,000 to $25,000. Over a decade, you would earn $110,000 to $323,000, which sounds like an OK return until you factor in inflation (the long-term rate in Australia between 1951 and 2023 is 4.9 per cent per annum) and tax, at which point you would have actually ended up with a negative return and fundamentally made yourself poorer than you were the decade before. The thing to remember with your savings is that over time they are being devalued and losing purchasing power. Inflation, after all, is the silent tax that keeps the middle and working classes working forever.

But let's say you invested that $500,000 instead and leveraged it into $2.5 million of assets. Now, to be conservative over the long term, let's say that it returns 7 per cent on your new asset base. Your new return would now be $175,000 per annum in capital growth alone. That's a 35 per cent return on your original asset base! This figure would also be compounding and would double your asset base within a decade, making you a whopping $2.4 million plus the cash flow from the rents increasing over time (see figure 4.1).

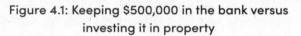

Figure 4.1: Keeping $500,000 in the bank versus investing it in property

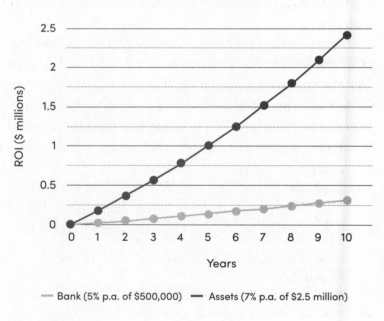

The wealthiest people always focus on how they can get rid of their money. Now, I know that probably sounds a bit odd, because who in their right mind wants to get rid of money? Isn't this book about making more of it? Of course it is. Let me explain.

What I mean is that they understand more than most that having money sitting around in their docile bank accounts will not improve their financial position in the long run, so they are perpetually searching for ways that they can make their money work harder for them. Generally, this means taking their cash out of these accounts and putting it into assets that will multiply that original money without them having to work for it themselves. This is a type of leverage where they use their current cash flow to increase and multiply their future cash flow.

They are always looking for ways to maximise their position, which means they never want to be sitting on too much cash or equity at any given point in time. This is because having money in the bank or under the mattress is a waste of potential returns. Instead, they will deploy that capital into an investment that will return more capital to them over time.

> **HOT TIP** All fiat currencies (government-issued currencies that are not backed by a commodity such as gold or silver) go to zero over time. All savings go to zero over time if not invested. This is simply the dollar losing value to inflation and silently robbing the middle class.

Most of us don't have stacks of cash just sitting around doing nothing, mind you. I don't mean that people are living week-to-week, but rather that many people don't have huge cash reserves they can simply inject into investment.

Even Elon Musk didn't have enough money at his disposal to buy Twitter, for example!

One of the most effective ways that you can multiply the money you have is by leveraging that phantom equity you have created in your assets (such as real estate). You have the opportunity to leverage equity whether you are extremely wealthy or just starting out.

I liken it to a snowball rolling down a hill. It starts off small and slow, but as it rolls down the hill it gets bigger, heavier and faster. The farther it rolls, the quicker it goes and the faster it grows.

Building wealth is the same: it starts slowly and feels like it takes forever, but the longer you do it, the more momentum you build. I know most people think they can 'get rich quick', and that can happen for an entrepreneur or one out of 100,000 businesses, but true wealth actually comes from getting rich slowly.

As I briefly mentioned earlier, one of the simplest ways for all people to create a leveraged portfolio is through real estate. Sure, in the beginning you will need to leverage your own savings to secure a loan to purchase that first property. After that, though, as long as you have chosen a property in a strategic location, you will likely never need to fork out so much of your own cash to purchase another property because you can use phantom equity instead.

Remember that you only had to work to save enough money for the first property, and then that property started to produce money on its own. This is what I call 'money while you sleep' because you make money from your assets around the clock.

If you repeat the process often enough, eventually you will reach a point when your investments are growing more than your everyday active income, and that is when you can choose whether you want to keep working in your job or retire younger and richer than you ever dreamed of.

### Investment tip

Phantom equity is extremely powerful. You can use it to turn a relatively small amount of money into a significant amount of wealth without having to trade your time for money. Be careful, though: you must know how to manage your phantom equity wisely so that it can continue to grow and make you money while you sleep. If you over-leverage, you could find that you don't have enough of an emergency buffer to cover your expenses. Interest rates can fluctuate over time, and you may find yourself needing to cover some unexpected costs in the short term. It's important to leverage safely and understand your LVRs (loan-to-value ratios) across your portfolio to manage the risks.

## Understanding debt

One of the biggest stumbling blocks for people who dream to create wealth is that they don't really understand the concept of debt at all. They view all debt as bad and don't recognise the difference between borrowing funds to generate more money and using credit that is attached to superfluous spending on credit cards or personal loans.

Now, I'm not saying that people shouldn't have a healthy respect for (rather than fear of) debt because you do need to understand the difference between good debt and bad debt. But having such a fear of debt, specifically mortgages, that you only ever buy one property when you could have purchased several is a sign that you don't understand how to leverage good debt to your advantage.

When most people think about debt, all they think about is enslaving themselves in a life of work. They believe that the only way they will ever be able to retire is to be debt-free… one day in the distant future. But when they do finally pay off their mortgage, they realise that using all of their income to pay down their debts means they have no savings to support their retirement, so they have to keep working for longer than they ever imagined. This is why so many people in their late 60s or early 70s are now either still working or merely surviving on the pension week to week.

As I've mentioned, debt can be good or bad depending on its intended use. Say someone goes out and gets a credit card, store card or one of those terrible buy now pay later loans (because a short-term loan is what they actually are) because they want to do some discretionary spending on clothes, shoes or a holiday that they can't really afford. Their desire for some instant gratification has led them to take on bad debt. The debt is not being used to purchase something that will increase in value, something that will make them wealthier; rather, it will keep them trapped in the workforce for longer while they pay off that liability.

Conversely, and importantly, if you borrow funds to invest in an asset that will make you more money over time, then you have created good debt, which is the kind that will improve your financial situation in the future.

HOT TIP There are two types of debt: good debt makes you more money and bad debt makes you poorer. If you don't understand the difference between the two, you will never retire younger or richer.

I have created millions of dollars over the past decade with very little effort on my part by regularly using good debt to my own financial advantage. My aim was never to get out of debt – it was to get into more of it so I could make more money from it. You see, the larger the asset base you create, the more wealth you will generate over the long term.

For example, 50 years ago, when an average house cost around $30,000 to $40,000, a middle-class person would probably buy one house and work 30 years of their lives to pay it off entirely. Remember, of course, that at the time $30,000 or $40,000 was a lot of money, and most families only had one person who worked full-time. However, by today's standards, it's about what a new car costs to purchase. Now, if that person just purchased that one house and paid it off, then today it may be worth about $1 million, giving them a net worth of $1 million; this is the situation for many baby boomers today. However, outside of the family home – which they would need to sell to realise the cash, after all – they probably have very little in savings to retire on.

Consider this, though: if we went back in time to that same person and asked them to buy the house next door at the same time, but not to pay off a single dollar during their entire working life, where do you think they would be financially today? Well, they would have two houses worth a total of $2 million and a debt of, say, $60,000 to $80,000, giving them a net worth of $1.92 to $1.94 million.

You can clearly see how they used the debt to their advantage by letting it devalue over time due to inflation and ended up a whopping $920,000 to $940,000 better off in the end. Even though they carry debt, it is now miniscule compared to their net worth. The best part about it is that if they had purchased even more real estate back then, they would have amassed even more wealth today.

This is the difference between paying off debt and using good debt to create more wealth for yourself.

By heading to yourpropertyyourwealth.com.au, you can find not only more information on my Investing Success course but also lots of useful information to continue your investment education.

### Investment tip

Debt is the most powerful tool with which to create wealth. You can turn a small amount of money into millions of dollars by using leverage. The key is to understand how to use debt safely.

Here are four tips to assess whether or not you're using debt correctly:

1. You're using debt to buy an asset that is likely to increase in value over time – no credit cards, personal loans or high-interest loans for luxuries.

2. You understand the benefits of using leverage but also the downside of leverage and its risks.

3.  You always have a strategy and the correct finance structure when using debt, and have an emergency fund to protect your wealth.

4.  You're managing your cash flows and equity levels while building your wealth to optimise your returns in a safe way.

## The game of money

It's no great secret that some of the richest entities in the world are those that lend people money to buy things. They are called banks.

Of course, the way that banks operate has changed drastically since our parents' and grandparents' days. Back then, the banks usually held all the cards, and it was a big deal whenever someone actually secured a home loan.

Times have changed. Lending practices are much more generous, and most households have two incomes that they can leverage now instead of one. One thing that hasn't changed very much, though, is that the people who understand the game of money and how it is played will generally wind up the richest.

The wealthiest understand that it is access to money that is always the most important, because if you don't have money then you can't leverage it to create more of it. However, most middle-class people view money as something that they physically have in their wallet or purses, or in their bank accounts in digital form. If they can physically see or feel their money, then they feel safe; but that safety is smoke and mirrors.

On the other hand, the wealthy always classify debt (the good kind) as money, because it is a tool that they can use to buy more assets that will make them even wealthier in the future.

One of the ways that many of us learned about money was through Monopoly. I'm sure you have stories about playing and someone getting so annoyed with the result that they stormed off or even threw the board in the air in frustration! This is like what happens on social media these days with the plethora of people complaining about how they can never change their financial situation, which is just not true for most income-earning people.

Let's use Monopoly as a metaphor to understand how the wealthy and the middle class view money. Say one player had to play using only the money that they had in front of them to buy assets, but another player could borrow against (or leverage) their properties to buy more properties – who do you think would win? Would it be the player who only has a property or two but lots of cash sitting in front of them, or the player who owns a number of streets and is forever collecting rent from players who land on their holdings?

Of course, it is the latter because of their superior rent intake and their ability to increase that cash flow by investing in more properties. The non-leveraged player will always be hamstrung by their inability to finance multiple properties because they weren't prepared to go into debt to do so. Plus, the leveraged player is fundamentally devaluing the savings of the other player by using debt to buy up more properties than they ever could dream of.

## Building momentum

One of the ways that I learned the true value of practising something until it becomes automatic, as well as tolerating and managing risk, was during my career as a freight train driver (and skydiving, which I discuss in the next chapter). Driving trains is another area in which you can use leverage to your advantage – which might sound a little odd, but let me explain.

When you're a freight train driver, you learn a route inside and out so that you know every part of the track. This is because sometimes you would experience 'black fog', which means you can't really see anything in front of you with the train lights on or off. We were trained to navigate every section of the route by using visual cues such as certain buildings, trees or specific geographic landmarks we could see out of the window at certain points of the journey so that we could effectively drive that train whether we could see in front of us or not.

People are also surprised by the fact that there isn't a steering wheel as such, and that every acceleration or deceleration has to be pre-emptively done long before the relevant section of the track. For example, if you go over a hill, you actually have to start backing off power once you've pulled halfway up the hill, because otherwise the back of the train is going to derail; plus, once you get to the top of the hill, you let the momentum take you down the other side.

The thing is, freight train drivers need to know how to do all of this without seeing it, which is why we practised so much, and learned from experts, before we ever started driving a route; it became automatic to us. The freight trains I was in charge of were 800 metres long across three locomotives and weighed north of 4000 tonnes, so you can understand why every driver must know their route automatically and practise for years before they are given the responsibility.

With a train that long and heavy, one of the most important skills you learn is momentum driving, because if you don't accelerate early enough you might not make it up a hill at all. Alternatively, you could get stuck there – possibly because you lost your bearings for a brief moment and didn't anticipate the route ahead – and then the entire network has to be shut down.

Momentum can help you cover long sections of the track if you know the journey ahead of you. I used to be able to drive for about 40 minutes without touching the accelerator once, just from my intricate knowledge of the route. Momentum driving is also a massive benefit to drivers of freight trains because it means that they are burning less fuel, which makes them happy because their employers often set fuel-efficiency targets linked to driver bonuses. And in the olden days, drivers would need to physically shovel coal to get to their destination, so momentum driving meant they could get there with less coal-shovelling. (This is very similar to the concept of using phantom equity instead of your own cash when investing in assets.)

The fuel that was used during your route was measured, so everyone knew who the good and bad drivers were. Plus, whoever was the most fuel-economical always got to the end of their route in the same time as the driver who used the most fuel.

Of course, there was no way you could be a momentum driver if you didn't know the route intimately. It was all about knowing what was ahead of you and putting into practice everything that you had learned during your years of training and experience.

I have carried over a lot of my past experiences, such as train driving, to building my wealth. What I have learned is that building wealth comes down to understanding the 'how' and then the 'why'. What follows then is the action.

From there, it's all about practice and time. It used to take about 15 years on average to learn the routes and become fully qualified to drive freight trains. It was all about trusting the process and imprinting the routes in my head until I could drive them in my sleep. Building wealth is no different! Once you understand these principles in depth and practise them, you will be well on your way to retiring younger and richer.

HOT TIP  Money is either costing you interest or it's saving you interest.

Basically, what I am saying is that debt is also money. It is costing you interest to have it, but all having money as savings is doing is saving you interest in some form.

One of the easiest ways to get your head around this concept is when you consider two different people who each buy a house. The first person, who has a scarcity mindset, decides to pay off that mortgage as quickly as humanly possible, which saves them interest. The other person, who has an abundance mindset, decides to repay the minimum loan amount so they can leverage the equity into more assets, which costs them interest but gives them the opportunity to make much more money from the assets over time than they would have lost in interest.

Understanding this concept is vital for anyone who wants to retire younger and richer. It's probably about now that you are thinking, *But isn't it a good thing to save my money and pay off the home loan?* and the answer is, well, you are doing that – sort of. Let me explain further.

## How to leverage phantom equity

To maximise the benefits of phantom equity, you need to repurpose the equity into more assets over time. The best way to do this is to pay down the loan on the property that you live in but then refinance that loan up to its maximum level so that you access that phantom equity to use as a deposit or down payment on more assets.

This scenario means that you are turning your savings into phantom equity by paying down (but not paying off) the home loan. It also means that you turn the non-deductible debt on your home loan into deductible debt on an investment property.

In this way, your assets act like a giant credit card: when you draw equity, you're getting access to credit, and if you spend that equity then you need to pay interest on it.

Another question you might have is, *But why use this leveraged equity when it's going to cost you interest to use it?* Well, this is the secret sauce of wealth creation, in my opinion. When you borrow funds (leverage) to invest in an asset, your equity costs you interest over time because you're increasing your loaned amount, but if you purchase another asset that increases in value at a greater rate than the interest cost of using that equity, then you will be making money off the bank's money.

**HOT TIP** If there is only one thing that you take away from this book, please make it this: if you take on debt to purchase good assets, they will increase in value at a greater rate than what the debt will cost you in interest, so you will end up better off than if you hadn't taken on the debt.

Let's take a look at an example of how this vital concept works in reality.

Imagine you have an asset that has increased in value by $100,000, and rather than doing nothing with it you decide you want to use this phantom equity to purchase another asset. Generally speaking, as long as you qualify for the additional finance, you will be allowed to do this by leveraging off the equity as well as the interest-rate cost that the bank has set at the time. In this example, let's use an interest rate of 5 per cent.

You decide to buy an income-producing asset like real estate that can cover the costs of the interest rate, which means you have low holding costs from the outset, plus it will make you money over time due to its value appreciation and increasing weekly rents. Fundamentally, the cost of borrowing the money is lower than the rate at which the asset you bought with that phantom money increases in value over time.

Say you buy an investment property for $800,000 and the cost of the property loan is an interest rate of 5 per cent per annum, which is $40,000. On top of the interest cost, you have property expenses of about $8000 per year, bringing the total to $48,000 per annum.

But that investment property is leased to tenants who pay you $45,000 in rent to live there, so your income on the property is therefore $45,000. It's an easy calculation to work out that you have a net loss of about $3000 per year, but there are potentially other factors, such as tax deductions or depreciation, which could see your loss turn into a positive of around $2000 per year.

So, that $800,000 property is already mostly paying its own way and not impacting your lifestyle much financially. However, what it is also doing is growing in value every year, which is where you will start to see significant changes to your overall net worth position.

If you have purchased a strategic property in a capital growth location, it might be increasing in value by 7 per cent per year, which means that in the first year it will have risen in value by $56,000. Even if it is costing you $3000 per year to hold, you are still $53,000 better off than you were before. Now, that figure is the same as what many people earn by trading their time for money every year, but you haven't had to physically work for it, have you?

If you hold that asset for long enough, it will make you a passive income, because the rent will rise higher than the interest rate and property expense costs, and it will also be compounding your wealth by an extraordinary 7 per cent every year.

Now, just imagine if you had half a dozen or more of these types of assets in your portfolio because you were able to make leverage your superpower. What would your wealth position be after a decade? What would it be after two decades?

It is important to note that interest rates will go up and down, and the property can go from positive cash flow to negative cash flow in a matter of months. Seems scary, right? Well, not if you already know that this could play out and you have figured out how you will deal with the situation.

For example, let's say that the interest rate on the $800,000 property went to 7 per cent and interest rate costs blew out to $56,000, plus $8000 for costs. That would mean your costs would be $64,000 per year and rent only $45,000. You would essentially be down $19,000 per year, and after tax and depreciation, say around $10,000. Most people would be freaking out!

Why hold an asset that is now costing you $10,000 per year? Well, remember that if growth is 7 per cent over the long term then the property's value would have risen $56,000 per year (which is compounding yearly, mind you). It may have cost you $10,000 that year, but you have still made $46,000 for the year in phantom equity, haven't you?

Another way to view it is in percentages from a break-even perspective. If the property costs you $10,000 per year because of interest rate rises, then it means that the property will need to grow in value by 1.25 per cent to break even over the long term. If you plan on building wealth for 15-plus years, do you think that the property will grow by at least that figure? Hell, it should at least keep up with long-term historical inflation of 2 to 3 per cent, not to mention that the rent will increase yearly and decrease the break-even point.

You see, I think of and run my portfolio as a business. Some years are great for cash flow and other years are not so great, but you don't just shut down the business after a bad year, do you? No, instead you rely on your cash flow through those times to see better times on the other side (drawing that cash flow from other sources, such as savings or equity).

When it comes to investing, don't just think it will be all rainbows and lollipops, because it won't. There is a reason that people never create true wealth: it's hard, and it takes a lot of education to understand how to play the game. This is why I have dedicated my life to teaching others the secrets of the wealthy.

## Top 3 takeaways

1.  The wealthiest people leverage their time, their money and their borrowed capital to increase their wealth position. They also never have money or equity sitting idly around doing nothing when they could use it to help grow their financial position.

2.  Creating phantom equity is one of the main ways the rich keep getting richer, and they understand how to leverage it to invest in even more assets.

3.  Understand that building wealth is like running a business. There will be good times and bad times, so you must understand your cash flow and your break-even points.

# Case study

## Using leverage to your long-term financial advantage

Dominique and Brooke were only 21 and working as nurses when they decided to buy their first property together. The couple decided they wanted to create a better financial future for themselves after watching the money struggles of their parents throughout their lives. The Sydney-based pair are strident savers, so as soon as they had enough money for a deposit, they purchased a unit in Gosford on the New South Wales Central Coast.

'As soon as we settled on it, we were ready to buy another one,' Dom recalls. 'We wanted to buy again already. We're very good at saving, let's say that. We live a simple life because we know where we're going and what we're doing.'

While that property has increased in value by about 30 per cent in the seven years since they bought it, Dom admits they could have purchased more strategically if they'd had some expert assistance. However, purchasing a property at all at just 21 – and on nursing salaries as well – is clearly something that should be celebrated!

Dom and Brooke connected with me and Sophie after spending some time following the Your Property Your Wealth educational updates on social media. Not long after, in early 2020, the pair – now with higher incomes due to career progression – purchased a three-bedroom house in Queensland's Moreton Bay region for $430,000. That property is worth about $750,000 at the time of writing and earns $480 per week in rent.

Because of this strong capital growth, as well as their desire to grow a portfolio sooner rather than later, I helped them buy another three-bedroom house in 2021 – this time in Brisbane's eastern suburbs – for $480,000. That asset has since grown in value by nearly $300,000 and achieves a weekly rent of $550.

Within the space of a year, Dom and Brooke achieved capital growth of $600,000 and were well on their way to achieving their dream of financial freedom.

But rather than rest on their laurels, with my help they secured another house in 2022, this time in North Perth, for $480,000, which has increased in value since settlement and is achieving $500 per week in rent. Before the age of 30, the pair have created a significant four-strong property investment portfolio as a result of their drive, diligence and money management.

'We're very driven and we know what we are doing. I think that's the main thing. And we have a lot of holidays as well. That's our two things in life – holidays and properties,' Dom says.

Dom and Brooke are currently rentvesters, but their longer-term plan is to start a family and buy their own home to live in, in Sydney but without a ridiculous mortgage, which was one of the main motivators for their investment strategy.

'How are we going to get around this problem of Sydney house prices? What are we going to do? I couldn't find answers, and then this seemed to be a good answer,' Dom says.

Dom says having an expert guiding them through location and asset selection made all the difference to their property investment purchasing experience. 'Now, I would never buy an investment property without a buyer's agent ever again. I think they just made it really easy. It was quite stressful when we bought Gosford by ourselves, and Daniel just teed the whole thing up for our second property purchase. If this is one of the most expensive things you'll ever buy in your life, why would you not do it with someone who's an expert? It just doesn't make sense. And Daniel's very good at haggling the price down, which we appreciate a lot!'

# Principle 5

# Tolerate and manage risk

I've known for a long time that I have a high tolerance for risk. That's why I used to skydive for 'fun' and also worked as a freight train driver for nine years!

Many people are conversative when it comes to risk, though, and especially when it comes to investing. They worry about taking on too much debt, and they worry about the risks involved in investments.

By this stage of the book, you understand more than most about how low-risk investing can be – as long as you have spent the time to educate yourself, worked on developing a wealth mindset, harnessed the value of your time, mastered consistency and made leverage your superpower.

The first three principles I just listed are probably the easiest to learn because they are mostly about working on yourself, without having to spend any of your own money or approach a lender so they can give you some of theirs. But it's those steps that stop most people from capitalising on their chances of retiring younger and richer because of their fear of the so-called 'risks' involved.

Of course, that sort of thinking is wrong, because there are strategies you can adopt that will manage the common risks associated with investing along the way.

## Business mindset

One of the first things that everyone must do is learn to treat their asset accumulation as a business. That means you have to focus on equity and capital growth but also on cash flow.

By adopting a business mentality, you will also be able to detach yourself emotionally from the process. With your business brain engaged, you need to ask yourself: do you have the cash flow and financial buffers to sustain your business? How are you going to protect the business?

> **HOT TIP** Building a portfolio is like building a castle. To protect your castle, you must build a moat around it. This is your emergency fund.

The bigger your portfolio, the bigger your emergency buffer needs to be to protect it. What does this mean in practice? It means that for each real estate asset you buy as an investment you must have emergency funds that will protect it. That figure for me is about $15,000 to $20,000 per property, but this can change depending on your risk tolerance. Each time you purchase another property using leverage, you must have another $15,000 to $20,000 that you keep in a separate account, preferably an offset account. For example, if you own five investment properties, you should have about $75,000 to $100,000 (five multiples of $15,000 to $20,000) in emergency funds that you can access when such things as urgent repairs are needed.

I bet many of you are thinking, *Well, that's alright for you, Daniel, but how am I going to save that amount of money to just have it sit there for a rainy day?* Well, the answer is that you don't need to do that at all! One of the most important strategies in this book is accessing funds that are available to you because of your investment decisions. As I mentioned in the previous chapter, creating your emergency fund is another way that phantom equity improves your finances and your wealth creation efforts.

Say you have bought two strategic investment properties, which have each grown in value by 7 per cent per year. You are ready to buy your third property, but you are committed to ensuring that you have the required level of emergency funds. This is when you refinance one of the properties to extract the required equity in cash that you then set aside in an account for your emergency funds. If you set aside emergency funds for your previous investment properties when you bought them, you should only need to tap into $15,000 to $20,000 to ensure that you have the right balance of emergency funds available for three properties (ideally $45,000 to $60,000), which is probably a small fraction of the total amount of equity available.

As you continue to build your portfolio, you can redeploy this strategy time and time again so that you never need to externally supply $20,000 for your emergency fund every time you buy another property.

### Investment tip

Your equity can act as a safety net in just the same way that cash can. Your goal is to protect your castle at all costs, because eventually a large enough castle will outperform your active income. This is when you will truly reach financial freedom.

Another reason to ensure you are managing the risks associated with investing by having emergency funds is to create a financial buffer to weather changing interest-rate environments.

As your portfolio (and your wealth) grows, the costs associated with holding these assets increase, including the compounding impact of rising interest rates on multiple properties. Rents will rise to cover these higher repayments over time, but there is often a lag, so you must have the funds available to cover the difference in the meantime.

One of the biggest stumbling blocks for many people when it comes to building a sizeable investment portfolio is that they don't want to even consider having to finance negative cash flow for a moderate period of time. They worry about 'affording' repayments when rates rise – because they don't understand using phantom equity, clearly – and would rather not take the 'risk', whereas I view it as a temporary issue that will be irrelevant years down the road when your portfolio has doubled in value.

As an example, you could be growing a $3 million portfolio which has a $30,000 negative cash flow each year. Of course, you can draw upon equity from your existing assets to help pay for this shortfall, and it's easy to understand that your overall wealth position will be significantly better in 10 years' time if you retain ownership of that portfolio, instead of letting $300,000 in costs over a decade – which are probably tax deductible and will likely be reimbursed in part by higher rents as well – scare you into not attempting to build this portfolio.

I mean, if you know how to control the $300,000 deficit – which, mind you, seems crazy and is something I have never seen – then don't let it deter you from holding a portfolio that only needs to grow by one per cent per year to break even. Given the likelihood that it will make you $2 million to $3 million over that same time period, you would have to have rocks in your head not to choose this option. Remember, if you understand the strategy, then the numbers aren't scary – they're actually exciting.

It's the misunderstanding of these 'risks' that really trips people up because they simply don't like things costing them money. That's part of the reason why so few people become financially free and even fewer can retire younger and richer than the generations before them.

## The day my parachute failed

As I mentioned at the start of this chapter, I used to love skydiving when I was younger. I loved the process of preparing for each jump but clearly also the adrenaline of flying through the air ready to pull the ripcord.

I have a much higher tolerance for risk than most people, but one day the worst thing that can happen when skydiving happened to me.

Most people don't understand that skydiving is actually a low-risk sport when you consider how many deaths there are on average per jump. Of course, it doesn't seem that way because you read about each death in the media, a bit like with shark attacks, but the reality is that you have more chance of dying driving your car to the airfield than jumping out of the plane.

The number-one most important thing in skydiving is procedure and risk management routines. You actually practise more on the ground than you ever skydive. I think I used to spend about 80 per cent of my skydiving time practising on the ground, so I was only actually jumping about 20 per cent of the time.

The reason for such a high percentage of training and practice is so that everything becomes automatic to you, which is vital if a problem arises when you are hurtling towards the ground at more than 100 kilometres per hour. During your practice on the ground, you go over and over the specifics of the jump as well as the various ways it might play out. You are pre-programming your mind to have an automatic, instantaneous response if needed.

I spent six months practising packing my parachute with a trainer. The second time that I packed it by myself, though, I somehow flipped the bag 180 degrees, which actually twisted every line over itself when I jumped.

I soon found myself in a real spin, but I was too low to be able to cut away and deploy the reserve parachute. I remember being confused about what was happening at first. I was falling at about 150 kilometres an hour and thought I was about to fall unconscious at any moment because I was spinning so quickly.

In a split-second, though, I automatically knew what I had to do to stop myself spinning. I reached up and grabbed the twisted lines above me, pulled them as far apart as I could and then tried to twist the opposite way by kicking out. I knew this was what I had to do because I had practised it every single day, so it was an automated response during a literal life and death situation.

Some people freeze in moments like these, but my brain told me to do the opposite of that by not freaking out and engaging my training step-by-step, which is a difficult thing to do in times of supreme stress, of course!

Though I managed to untwist the lines in time, I still hit the ground pretty hard – but I was alive to tell the tale. This is because learning the process and practising it over and over again allowed me to have an automatic response to solve the problem.

That same day, I carefully repacked my parachute, went back up and jumped again, because I knew if I didn't then the fear may have manifested in my brain and I would have never skydived again.

## Different investment options

During your wealth creation journey, you will no doubt consider, and engage, a number of different investment strategies and asset classes. I have mostly spoken about property in this book, but you could also choose to invest in cryptocurrencies or the share market. Any investment vehicle that has the potential to improve your financial situation, without it being pure speculation, can be useful as long as you go into it with your eyes wide open.

I spent the entire previous chapter talking about leverage because it is a sound and low-risk technique for investing in real estate assets; however, the same can't be said for crypto or stocks. Leverage can cause all manner of problems with these riskier types of assets because they are more volatile than property, which has a proven history of stable capital growth over the decades.

One of the biggest risks of using leverage to purchase stocks is the volatile nature of share prices, which can jump up and down sharply on any given day for reasons that you as a lowly shareholder cannot control. Just imagine, then, if you had leveraged your way into those shares and their value plummeted so that you were in negative-equity territory in the space of a few days or even hours. Most people would probably freak out and sell, which would compound their losses even more.

Real estate assets are tangible, illiquid and much less prone to sharp rises or falls in value – especially if those properties have been strategically selected to maximise their future capital growth. That's why I believe real estate is the lowest-risk investment you can make.

### Investment tip

Bricks-and-mortar real estate is an asset but also a necessity for every human. It's an asset that has stood the test of time and will continue to do so forever. It's so trusted that the system allows you to leverage up to 95 per cent of its value, making it one of the best assets to protect your wealth from inflation over time. It's the ideal set-and-forget asset.

Another popular investment vehicle, of course, is crypto, which is one of the highest-risk options out there in my opinion. That's not to say it doesn't suit some people, though, as long as they have a high tolerance for risk and completely understand what the end result may be for them – a big gain or a big loss.

I have invested in crypto myself, but I always did so with the mindset – and the financial capability – that if I lost the funds I invested then I could live with that. No one should ever invest in such a high-risk venture without being able to kiss that money goodbye and never look back with regret.

While I am essentially gambling (in an educated way) on crypto, I am able to do so because I have excess funds available to me that I won't miss if they disappear. However, when I make money from crypto (which earned me $1.8 million at one point), I automatically transfer that money back into my portfolio (or my emergency funds account). The way I view shares and crypto as investment options is that I always intend to be in those markets over the short-term only, with any profits recycled back into the safety of bricks and mortar as soon as possible so that I can preserve the wealth I have created.

As you are learning, the creation of wealth is one thing, but you also need to master the preservation of wealth so you can retire younger and richer or pass on your wealth to the next generation. There is no better asset than real estate for new investors, in my opinion, because of the potential for solid returns year after year, which you can leverage to create more wealth. As time goes on, you may want to invest in different asset classes – I certainly have – but my results have never been as spectacular or linear in other asset classes as in trusty old bricks and mortar.

Consider this as an example: say you decide to invest $100,000 in the stock market, maybe a managed fund of blue-chip stocks of some sort. After a year, the fund records a 10 per cent value uplift, which is actually pretty good. But that's only a $10,000 return on your $100,000 investment. At that rate, after a decade of compounding 10 per cent per annum you may wind up with a $170,000 return, more than doubling your initial investment. But imagine if you had invested that $100,000 into a $600,000 property instead: if it grew in value by 7 per cent per annum, after the first year you would have made $42,000 – more than four times as much as your share investment. After 10 years, that property may be worth $1.2 million, which is a value uplift of $600,000 – over three times the result that you may have achieved with shares (see figure 5.1). The numbers simply don't lie!

Figure 5.1: Compound returns of $100,000 invested in the stock market versus as a down payment on a $600,000 property

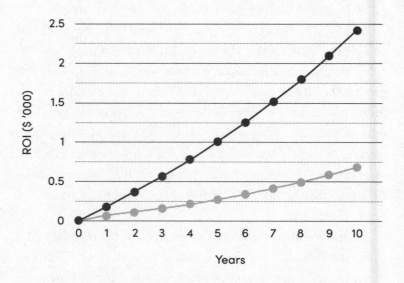

── Stock market (10% p.a. of $100,000) ── Property (7% p.a. of $600,000)

In mid-2022, I had a client who achieved a 33 per cent cash-on-cash return on a property in just four months! Their $100,000 initial deposit resulted in a value increase to $166,000 in four months. No other asset class can compete with that in a safe manner, in my experience.

## Market scaremongering

Do you remember back in the early days of the COVID-19 pandemic when property prices were predicted to fall by 30 per cent?

While the pandemic was a scary and unusual time for us all, what wasn't unusual was the influx of doomsday property merchants as soon as we closed the doors to our homes during the very first lockdowns. Headline after headline screamed at us that real estate Armageddon was nigh, so as well as worrying about the virus many people started to fear that their wealth creation efforts were on the line.

The forecasters who dared to offer a different scenario were trolled mercilessly online because, clearly, they were talking nonsense. What would they know, the masses cried!

Of course, those few learned individuals were proven right. They had done their research and understood how markets generally perform in times of trouble (which is usually a sharp drop in interest rates to shore up the economy). The extraordinary price growth that many property markets around the globe recorded during 2021 in particular was not just to do with interest rates but also a reduction in supply, as well as a heady rush of buyers keen to park their money in the safest asset of all!

Alas, some people were scared by these alarmist forecasts at the start of the pandemic (which turned out to be false, by the way), and so they sold their holdings or chose not to purchase during the soft market conditions in 2020. These two options would prove to be the worst possible financial decisions they could have made at the time.

I guess the point I'm trying to make with this little history lesson is that following stories from populist media outlets will never give you an accurate picture of what is happening in markets. That is not what their stories are about, anyway. These media outlets want to attract as many eyeballs as possible so their advertisers are happy and they can keep their jobs, too. That's why you often see opposing viewpoints of the market being published at about the same time, sometimes from the same news outlet!

The forecasters who were proven right during the pandemic were those who used history as their guide. While none of us know what tomorrow will bring, real estate has been transacted for hundreds of years, so it has a long history of data to draw conclusions from.

One of the most important things that you can do when starting on your journey to wealth is to accept that it is likely to take time – a decade or even two – to get there. This means that the short-term fluctuations, or screaming headlines, should cause you no bother whatsoever, because today doesn't matter – what matters is the very distant future. This is another risk-management technique that you need to learn. You must always focus on the horizon, rather than be spooked by short-term factors that may only have a temporary impact on your wealth. By focusing on the future, you will be able to manage and tolerate any so-called risks that are causing other people to second-guess their financial positions or their investment plans and dreams.

According to the *Aussie Progress Report* commissioned by Aussie Home Loans and produced by CoreLogic, the price of real estate in Australia has skyrocketed over the three decades from December 1991 to December 2021 (see figure 5.2, overleaf):

- Australian house values increased 414.6 per cent and unit values increased 293.1 per cent. The 30-year annualised growth for houses was 5.6 per cent and for units was 4.7 per cent.

- The value of dwellings across the combined capital cities increased 414.9 per cent, and the value across the combined regions increased 278 per cent. The 30-year annualised growth was 5.6 per cent across the combined capitals and 4.5 per cent across the combined regional market.

- The highest increase in values over the 30-year period was across Sydney, where capital growth was 475.1 per cent and annualised growth was 6 per cent. The lowest capital growth returns in the period were across regional WA, where dwelling values rose 207.5 per cent and annualised growth was 3.8 per cent.

What is really telling in this report is the fact that there was an ebb and flow of real estate prices throughout that period, with seven periods of sustained increase in values at the national level and seven periods of decline.

## Figure 5.2: Rolling annual change in CoreLogic Home Value Index of Australian dwelling values

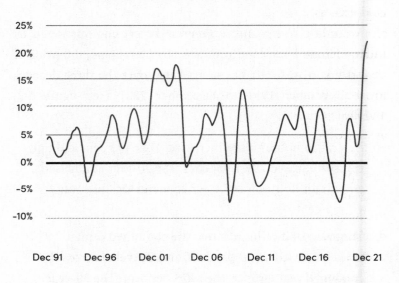

Source: CoreLogic

The research found that the value increases over the course of these cycles had an average length of 41 months, with average cumulative growth of 34 per cent. Comparatively, periods of peak-to-trough decline lasted 12 months on average, with an average fall in values of 4.3 per cent. The most recent national housing market upswing at the time of writing, which commenced in October 2020, lasted 17 months to February 2022, with national values increasing 27 per cent over that period of time.

Of course, we all have short memories when it comes market cycles, and so many younger entrants into the real estate market may think that the pandemic property boom was the most spectacular in history; this research proves that it actually wasn't when it comes to longevity. It pales in comparison to the period between September 1995 and January 2004 – so, almost eight-and-a-half years – when the national Home Value Index increased for 95 of the 101 months. (Interestingly, this period was marked by a relatively low cash-rate environment for the time, averaging 5.5 per cent between December 1994 and December 2004; prior to December 1994, the cash rate had averaged 8.5 per cent.)

So, what does this mean for the wealth positions of anyone who purchased an affordable (for the time) property or two back in 1991? Well, nowadays they are generally property millionaires and then some. Consider that in 1991 the median dwelling value of the 'middle market' was about $114,000. Three decades later, the median dwelling value was nearly $710,000 – an increase of nearly 407 per cent! Anyone who owned two or more of these 'middle market' properties would be sitting on a portfolio worth at least $1.4 million, likely with no mortgages (or very small mortgages) given the downward effect of inflation on debt.

Now, hopefully, you can see why I have devoted an entire chapter to tolerating and managing risk. It is paramount if you want to retire younger and richer. Real estate is the lowest-risk asset class out there, and the potential to create significant wealth is there – as long as you keep your eye on the prize.

## Top 3 takeaways

1.  The smartest investors treat their portfolios as businesses, which means they always ensure they have adequate cash flow to keep it running and finance any unexpected expenses such as emergency repairs.

2.  If you decide to invest in more risky ventures, always adopt a short-term mindset, with any returns being immediately transferred into real estate or your emergency fund so that you can preserve and grow your wealth.

3.  Don't be drawn into market scaremongering or short-term fluctuations that will have very little impact over the long term. Real estate has a proven history of capital growth within a low-risk environment.

# Case study

## A strategic plan for a better life

When Christina migrated to Sydney from Lebanon, she knew she wanted to create a new life for herself. She set about working hard in the finance industry so she could afford to buy a property one day. Her desire to have a better financial life than her parents had was a key goal because she had watched them work very hard since she was a young child.

'I wanted to have something, to have a backup plan, just in case I lost a job or something. So I kept working and saving on the side. And I kept thinking, *Oh, I need to put a deposit on a house*, but obviously the Sydney market was so expensive, I couldn't afford it,' she recalls.

In 2017, then in her 30s and priced out of the Sydney market, she decided to buy a house in regional Victoria after saving an impressive $70,000 for the deposit and spending time there with relatives. Afterwards, though, she started concentrating on property investment education and realised that she might need some assistance to maximise her income in the future as a single woman.

A few years later, Christina bought a house in Brisbane and continued along her path of educating herself and seeking out property investment experts, while also working two jobs from time to time to grow her savings even more.

After following my Instagram, she reached out to the Your Property Your Wealth team in 2021 and the conversation progressed to deciding to work together.

'You know how things click and you feel you're comfortable talking to a person, and then they're actually very transparent in the way that they transmit information?' Christina remembers. 'It was Daniel's journey as well, the fact that he actually made himself, and that's what attracted me the most – because I was the same. I didn't have any support from my parents. The fact that he made himself from scratch and is actually willing to share that knowledge instead of keeping it to himself, it just shows that he's a genuine person.'

By August of that year, I had helped Christina buy a house in the eastern suburbs of Brisbane for $530,000, which achieved 36 per cent capital growth in just 18 months and is zoned for medium development as well. Christina's experience was so positive that within a few months she decided to add to her portfolio again, this time with a house on the northern side of Brisbane, which increased in value by nearly 10 per cent in less than a year.

By mid-2022, there were still some Brisbane markets that offered sound investment prospects, as long as you knew where to look and what to look for. This is what I did for Christina again, and my team helped her secure another eastern suburbs house, which experienced a 5 per cent value uplift in just three months.

Throughout the past year, Christina has been committed to building her property investment portfolio as well as continuing to learn every step of the way.

'I recommended Daniel to a lot of my friends and family, and they're all happy with him. When you trust someone, that's when you feel like you want to recommend them to others, and he hasn't failed me. I just feel he has a lot of great knowledge, especially knowing where to buy and which markets are picking up, which I don't think I could have done myself.'

## Principle 6

# Create compounding wealth

As I mentioned earlier, Albert Einstein is famously reported to have said, 'Compound interest is the eighth wonder of the world. He who understands it, earns it... he who doesn't... pays it.' The wealthiest people not only understand the power of compounding, they have actively become rich because of it, too.

Throughout this book I have provided examples of how growing wealth is as much about leverage and time as it is about anything else. Once you have begun your wealth creation journey and have committed to retiring younger and richer, then you must follow through with your plan to multiply your assets and your income streams.

And the more years that your investments have time to grow in value, the richer you and your family will eventually be – because of compounding.

## Multiple income streams

If you think back to the first principle, about generational wealth, you will recall that many of the world's wealthiest families started with one business idea – whether that was a hotel, a department store or a confectionery item – but over the decades, as their businesses and personal wealth grew, they continually added businesses or products to their balance sheets.

What they were doing was multiplying their ability to achieve compounding income and asset growth in the future, which is why many of these families now have net worths of billions upon billions of dollars. Sure, if they had retained their original businesses and never added to or expanded their offerings, they would probably still have done better than most, but their family wealth would probably have withered away after a generation or two.

It will not surprise you at this point that the same concept goes for real estate investment – it is the compounding effect of owning a number of properties that can make a huge difference to your overall wealth position.

Just remember those statistics from the previous chapter: dwelling values in Australia's capital cities increased nearly 415 per cent over the past three decades. This means that people who started investing in the early 1990s and had the means to leverage their first property into half a dozen, as an example, are likely to have a net worth of about $3 million or more, all using the low-risk asset that is real estate as the vehicle.

Before you argue, 'But Daniel, the average house back then was only $115,000 or so', you must consider that price alongside the average full-time weekly wage at the time, which was about $524, according to the Australian Bureau of Statistics. In May 2023, the average weekly wage was about $1838 per week.

Some property investment detractors also will argue that property prices have increased more than wages over that period of time, and they would be correct, but part of the reason for that is the fact that women are more active in employment now, so it is now the norm rather than the exception for two incomes to be assessed in home loan applications. This has increased the borrowing power of property buyers and therefore has had an inflationary impact on real estate prices.

### Investment tip

Every generation thinks that property is too expensive. The problem is that people never understand that the dollar is losing value over time. It's not that the house got better over the past 20 years; in fact, it got worse! The dollar lost its value against the asset.

When buying property, you stop the clock on the dollar's loss of value. You're betting that fiat currency will devalue over the long term. This is why scarce assets like real estate appreciate in value against money supply over time.

I started my property investment and wealth creation journey when I was 19, and by the time I was 32 I owned a 16-property-strong portfolio worth $20 million.

However, four years earlier my portfolio numbered nine properties and was valued at $5 million. This means that in the space of just four years, my portfolio increased in value by $11 million and my net worth also skyrocketed to $10 million. Having multiple properties in my portfolio just before a market cycle boom meant that my net worth was able to rise rapidly because of the uplifting effect of compounding across my assets. This shows the positive effect of compounding on multiple assets pretty well, doesn't it?

One thing that made these spectacular results a possibility for me was starting when I was younger than most. By now you know my backstory, but anyone who can start on their wealth creation journey at a young age will have more time on their side to maximise their financial success.

I believe that anyone who has the drive, determination and financial capability to begin working towards their investment dreams should do so as soon as they can. Not only will it provide more time for compounding to work its magic, but it also means that you will have more latitude when it comes to the liability side of your balance sheet, as well as being able to enjoy the fruits of your labour while you are younger.

## The early fruits of your labour

One of the trickiest elements of wealth accumulation over the long term is that many people are fixated on the end goal, which is a good thing, but they forget to enjoy their lives at the same time. Personally, I don't see the point of scrimping and saving and doing deal after deal for decades if it means that you are surviving on baked beans, spam or peanut butter and jam sandwiches for years.

When you start out on your investing journey, sure, you will need to watch every dollar so that you can save the funds required for your first investment deposit. As you know, from when I was 16 I saved nearly half of my apprentice wages, while paying board to my parents, to squirrel away enough money for a deposit. I also had to sell my reasonably nice car and buy a 'bomb' so I could finish construction of my first house at just 19 years old. But that first asset set the ball rolling for every single asset after it, which means the sacrifices I made were definitely worth the financial pinch (and teenage car pride) at the time.

It's with this principle that my personal strategy probably deviates from many other wealth creation advisers, because I believe that if you start investing early enough – and purchase the right type of properties in the right places for the right prices – then, after about a decade, you will probably be in a position to reward yourself.

This is the opposite of how most people operate when they are trading their time for money throughout their lives, especially those who move up the ranks in their careers and start earning higher salaries. What generally happens is that as they earn more money by trading their time for money, their expenses rise to meet their new income level. You might be surprised that some of the highest-paid professionals out there don't have an investment strategy or portfolio at all. Sure, they may live in a nice house with Insta-worthy views and drive the latest BMW or Mercedes Benz, but behind the scenes they are paying for all of those nice things via huge mortgage repayments and personal loans.

Of course, I'm not saying they don't deserve those things – they may have toiled away for years in their career and at university to get to where they are – but if they decide to purchase these sorts of status symbols as soon as they start earning high incomes, they may never have enough funds left over to invest in anything.

This can also be a danger for younger workers who might be earning a median income, perhaps as a tradesperson or even a realtor, because it's during your 20s and even 30s that appearance counts the most. This is why we see tradies going out and spending $80,000 via personal loans on the latest four-wheel drive or utility vehicle, and we see sales agents driving around in the most popular status vehicle – perhaps a Tesla – using a novated lease, which lenders don't like to see on anyone's expense column, to tell the truth. Plus, they make the repayments on these after tax, which is why these types of loans or leases hang around for years and years, increasing the total interest payable or the final balloon payment.

These types of depreciating assets can provide lots of happy feelings for your ego, but the loans or leases that you are using to pay for them are going to be a huge drain on your potential borrowing capacity every time you apply for finance. It was this realisation that motivated me to drive about in that $1500 car for years and years until it finally died one day.

People who are a decade or more into their strategic investment journey and have accumulated a reasonable net worth behave quite differently. Let me explain further.

My hard rule is I am allowed to spend up to 10 per cent of my net worth every few years on something tangible, like a new car, caravan or even a Rolex watch – but not on holidays, which have to be financed out of my regular cash flow. Why? Well, it's because you can sell those tangible products at some time in the future. You may not sell them for the price you paid for them (or they may be worth more if they are rare and in demand), but at least you will get something back for them, unlike an exotic holiday.

Now, the caveat to this system is that you must only ever allow yourself to indulge in these purchases if your assets are compounding in value faster than your liabilities. In the beginning this may take up to a decade, but after that you may be able to dip into your phantom equity every three or four years.

Let's consider the following example. Say that your net worth is $2 million after a decade, because your original portfolio cost $2 million but it is now worth $4 million. If you asked me whether you could access some of those funds to purchase, say, a new vehicle, I would generally tell you that you could – as long as the growth projections for the portfolio also supported this purchase.

Using my 10 per cent maximum model, this may mean you could withdraw up to $200,000 of your phantom equity. Of course, you may choose to only spend $50,000 of it and park the rest in your emergency funds account. Just because you can spend it doesn't mean you should, after all.

Some people will argue that this would have a detrimental impact on your overall wealth position in the decades ahead, but I believe it will be negligible if you have time on your side. If you have a $2 million net worth when you are 35, for example, and you decide to withdraw $200,000, your net worth will obviously be reduced to $1.8 million. However, the beauty of compounding is that if your portfolio compounds in value by 7 per cent annually, that $200,000 will be returned to your balance sheet within 18 months.

Another bonus of using this strategy is that the funds you are accessing are generally tax-free or are being repaid by the compounding effect of price growth on your portfolio.

## My dream car purchase

As I mentioned earlier, when I was a teenager I promised myself that I would buy a Lamborghini one day. Of course, most of my mates just laughed at me, because such an expensive vehicle was simply out of the realms of possibility for us working-class folk.

Even though they made fun of me, and I did spend years driving around in a crappy old Daihatsu Feroza and a Kia Rio, I never let go of that dream and always had it as one of my manifestations that I diligently worked towards.

I never gave myself a deadline to achieve this goal. Rather, as I've mentioned, I always told myself that I just wanted to own a Lamborghini before I died, which gave me about 60 years or even 70 years to achieve it! No pressure at all, really.

But as I grew my portfolio and launched my business, with each step I knew that I was edging closer to the day when I could buy a Lamborghini with cold hard cash.

Because I had created a nine-property-strong portfolio by 2019 – generally while earning average wages – that meant that when the property boom came during the pandemic, I was in the best financial position possible to experience the wondrous impact of compounding growth. In fact, my net worth skyrocketed by $4 million in just three years! Because I follow the same strategies that I am outlining and recommending to you, this meant that I had about $700,000 of phantom equity that I could realise (10 per cent of the $7 million).

Apart from extracting funds from time to time to build up my emergency buffer, I had never dipped into my net worth to take on this sort of liability, let alone one of the world's most expensive vehicles. But I had no need to feel guilty, because I knew I had worked my butt off to achieve more by the time I was 31 than most people do in a lifetime. Plus, I still had time on my side for compounding and rental growth to repay those funds.

I am happy to say that in April 2022, I went and purchased a steel-grey Lamborghini for $400,000 using my phantom equity and having my assets cover this cash withdrawal. In the year leading up to that purchase, my portfolio experienced around $2 million of growth, so the $400,000 was a drop in the ocean compared to the phantom equity that I had created.

It took me 15 years to achieve my dream because I was prepared to drive a clapped-out old rust bucket for years, while also living in a garage for a time, so I could save enough money to buy assets that would one day allow me to do something as crazy as purchase my very own Lamborghini.

## Techniques that work

You should now be starting to imagine what your life might look like in 10, 20 or even 30 years' time.

Of course, we all look to mentors to help guide us to success, whether that be financial or in our careers, which is why it's so vital that you be selective with the people you trust your future with. Unfortunately, in every industry there are people who don't have your best interests at heart, as all they really want to do is sell you the latest get-rich-quick scheme or try to convince you that a particular location is destined to be the next big thing for property investors.

While I have spent a fair bit of time talking about mindset and wealth creation principles in this book, the insights regarding property investment are tried and true – and have been adopted successfully by many people in history.

### Investment tip

Understanding that all money is debt and that you either earn interest or pay interest is very powerful. Then, understanding how the wealthy take on liabilities and grow their wealth tax-free is a game changer.

The $30 million question, though, is: how do you even get to the starting blocks? If you earn moderate wages but have big dreams, how do you achieve what may seem at the outset to be impossible?

I know it can be done because I am living and breathing proof of it. I am from a working-class background, from a blue-collar part of western Sydney, but I have a net worth of $10 million and recently bought a $400,000 Lamborghini and my dream home on the northern beaches of Sydney on the water, a far stretch from where I came from.

And I managed to achieve all of this because of the six principles that I have happily shared with you in this book.

That said, there are a couple of basic fundamentals to follow if you want to make your wealth-creation dreams come true. By applying these, you will ensure that you are setting yourself up for success from the first day that you decide you want to retire younger and richer than anyone in your family has ever done before.

## 1. Implement a savings strategy

You are probably wondering how I managed to save $34,000 when I started out earning $254 per week. Most people just don't think it's possible, but it is – as long as they are dedicated and have a structured plan.

Automatically transfer a minimum of 20 per cent of your wages or salary into a separate savings account as soon as you get paid. In the beginning you will be stress-testing your lifestyle to see how you can manage this reduction in money at your disposal. You may need to make sacrifices to ensure you can save 20 or even 30 per cent of your income from each pay period.

The separate savings account should ideally be with a different bank as well so that you can't easily transfer the funds back again. That savings account should not have a bank card attached to it, either.

It is easier to save more when you are younger because younger people don't have as many expenses as older people, such as child-related expenses, for example. However, if you are older, don't let this stop you; regardless of your age, you will never be able to save the funds that are required to invest unless you set up an automated saving system like this.

## 2. Use different banks

The days of the big banks having a stranglehold on the banking sector are long gone. Plus, there has been steep growth in the finance broking sector, which gives every person more choice when it comes to how they secure funds to finance their investment.

A mistake that some inexperienced investors make is to use the same lender for all of their borrowings. While they may think that loyalty is good, trust me, it's not, with current borrowers generally not getting deals as good as those that are available to new customers.

It's important to recognise that when you have all your borrowings with one bank, then it's them and not you who has the balance of power. Say you are looking to borrow again but you already have $2 million in loans with them; it only takes one person on their side of the ledger to wonder whether they are exposing themselves to too much risk and you're knocked back with a stroke of the pen.

Now, you should be able to see how the opposite can be true when you share your lending requirements around a number of different banks. Not only can you tap into deals offered to attract new borrowers, but as long as your portfolio stacks up and your cash flow is solid, they are more likely to say yes because they don't have financial responsibility for your current borrowings.

Another strategy that I like, which is recommended for people who are keen to build a portfolio of five or more properties, is to use diverse types of lenders for your borrowings. Consider using a bigger, more traditional bank to extract equity – say, from your home – because they have tougher servicing calculators. Use the equity for deposits, and then go to the smaller second- and third-tier lenders to keep purchasing more properties, because they are generally more agreeable to financing investors.

There may come a time when you will need to consider a third-tier or less traditional lender to secure finance for, say, your fifth or six property. Now, I'm not suggesting that you are using these lenders because your numbers don't stack up. Rather, it's about managing the risks that banks see when investors start to accumulate a reasonable-sized portfolio: if you go into too much debt with a single lender, they may worry about your ability to service the loans.

By the time most investors have created a five- or six-property-strong portfolio, enough time has elapsed for the power of capital growth to start to shine, along with rising cash flow from rents. This means that you should be able to refinance with top-tier lenders some of the properties you originally financed using second-tier lenders, at which point you can withdraw some of that phantom equity to potentially purchase another property or to put towards your emergency fund.

*

By employing these two simple strategies at the beginning and throughout your investment journey, you will be setting yourself up for success and ensuring that your financial destiny is in your hands and your hands alone.

## Top 3 takeaways

1. The richest people understand that compounding growth will make them even wealthier, so they buy more assets and create multiple income streams to make the most of this 'eighth wonder of the world'.

2. I don't believe you have to wait until you are retired to enjoy the fruits of your investment labour. Rather, as long as the value of your assets is increasing at a greater rate than your associated liabilities, you can use some of your phantom equity to buy something tangible like a new car or boat.

3. By being selective with your mentors and following the six principles and proven techniques in this book, including adopting a simple saving scheme and using a variety of different lenders for your borrowings, you can retire younger and richer.

# Case study

## A portfolio primed for compounding capital growth

Fewer than one per cent of all Australians own five investment properties, and Diana and Tyler are among that small percentage at just 31 years of age. The Adelaide-based couple are the proud owners of a $4.2 million, five-property-strong portfolio across three different states after adding three properties in less than a year. Diana, a geologist, and Tyler, an engineer, wanted to make the most of their incomes while they were young, which saw the couple supercharge their portfolio in 2022.

After buying two Torrens-title cottages in Adelaide in 2020, the couple was keen to keep adding to their portfolio but found themselves missing out because of the strong market conditions at the time. Diana had spent the past few years educating herself on property investment strategies and also started following my social media posts, which prompted the couple of reach out to my team.

'We did a bit of research on Adelaide areas, and we had selected a few areas we wanted to purchase in, but it was just too tricky. The market was so hot. That's why we went down the path of the buyer's agent, with the intention of then being able to get the property more easily, because we just kept missing out,' Diana recalls.

The couple are diligent savers, so they had plenty of funds to help finance another investment property or two – or three, as it turned out!

In early 2022 I helped them secure a three-bedroom house on the eastern side of Brisbane that increased in value by $160,000 in less than a year and only needed a quick cosmetic renovation to see its weekly rent soar from $450 to $620. The strong capital growth, coupled with their savings and high incomes, meant the couple was ready and able to buy another property within a few months, which is when I helped them secure another eastern-suburbs house in Brisbane that also had development potential.

'It's an 800-plus-square-metre block with the option to split to the rear and put a driveway up. We're retaining the front property, so we don't have to knock anything down. We'll be building that probably next year. We've always wanted to do it, but I don't think we were thinking of building for at least 10 years,' Diana says.

After construction, the two dwellings will likely have a combined value of $1.6 million versus costs of about $1.3 million, while the front house is currently rented as well.

The Brisbane market started to feel a little overheated in some areas in the second half of 2022, so my focus shifted to desirable suburbs in Perth instead. The significant equity growth that Diana and Tyler had created from their two recent purchases meant they were soon interested in adding a fifth property to their growing investment portfolio.

In September of 2022, my team assisted them to secure a house one suburb back from the beach in North Perth, which is located in a high-capital-growth area and is considered a set-and-forget investment since it had already been renovated.

This last property meant that by the end of 2022, Diana and Tyler had created a $4.2 million property portfolio while still in their early 30s. The couple's long-term plan is to replace their incomes, but in the meantime they have prioritised making the most of their cash flow while they are young and child-free.

Diana doesn't believe they would have ever tried, or even considered, buying multiple properties interstate in less than a year themselves.

'My husband would've gone around in circles because he would want to analyse every bit of the data! Even to purchase in the short timeframe, that was a difficult thing for him to do,' Diana recalls. 'Our long-term goal is to keep as many as we can. We do want to buy our dream home at some point, which in Adelaide is probably something like the $2 million mark, and we will be patient to achieve that in the future.'

# Conclusion

# Your time is now!

I hope that at this very moment you are beginning to believe that you, too, can retire younger and richer.

At the start of this book, you probably had your doubts, didn't you? But as you have learned by now, the power to create, grow and retain wealth is yours – and you have already progressed past the first step, which is understanding the key principles that can help you achieve financial success.

Fundamentally, my six principles can become your personal money blueprint, because by understanding and implementing each one of them you can instigate the necessary financial and mindset changes to start your wealth creation journey.

Retiring younger and richer can mean different things for each and every person. For one person, 'richer' might mean having enough cash flow from their investments to work part-time or not at all, while for another person it might mean owning $10 million worth of assets and creating significant generational wealth for their family. For one person, 'younger' might mean in their 30s, while for another person it might mean in their 50s or beyond.

Indeed, many people will opt to retire from their day jobs to concentrate solely on their investment strategy once their income streams allow them to do so. The key here is to follow these six principles to create substantial wealth so you have the choice of whether you want to keep working or not!

Let's do a little refresher on everything you have learned so far.

## Success steps

It's a sad fact that many people will wind up in exactly the same financial place that they started off in, and that their parents and grandparents started off in, too. While it is easier for people to transfer from working to middle class in today's society, it can still be difficult to make the leap from there to being truly wealthy.

The main reason for this is that most people spend their lives trading their time for money, which leaves precious few hours in the day, let alone brainpower, to learn about investment strategies or actually take educated and insightful action.

Many people also never save enough money to take the first step and purchase an asset, or they buy the wrong type to start off with, which prevents them from ever reaching a point where they can leverage it.

Even those who do may struggle to do anything else because they just don't have the mindset or the knowhow to take things further.

## Principle 1: Build generational wealth

Any family that has true generational wealth started out some-where, usually with a forebear doing something entrepreneurial that got the ball rolling. That person may have had a natural money blueprint that they instinctively followed. Nowadays, that is something you can learn.

Anyone who has a dream to create wealth should follow the concept of birds of a feather flocking together. Surround yourself with the types of people who have achieved what you want to achieve and who support and understand your financial dreams.

You should also work through the four wealth phases, which are accumulation, breathing space, re-accumulation and consolidation.

## Principle 2: Create a money mindset

There is no question that mindset matters if you ever want to achieve anything outside of the norm, but merely thinking about success won't change a thing.

I have always been a strong believer in the power of manifes-tation as it allows me to think my way through a problem to a solution, and it always enables me to believe that I can achieve the outcome. Just remember how I manifested my desire to one day own a $10 million house and how I created the steps for myself to achieve that goal.

However, to achieve any goal you must eventually take action, which is the tipping point for many people who dream about certain things – buying an expensive car, writing a book – but never actually do anything to make it a reality.

The wealthiest people also have a mindset that sees them playing to win and never playing to not lose. They have an abundance mindset rather than a scarcity mindset, and they have put in the work to create pathways for financial success.

## Principle 3: Master consistency and maximise your time

The saying 'practice makes perfect' is vital for anyone who wants to retire younger and richer. Not only must you understand the key principles inside and out, you must also consistently work towards achieving your goals by successfully completing each step along the way. Remember, habits are the actions that create the outcome.

You must always be persistent and never let naysayers make you reconsider your goals and dreams. This includes never taking no for an answer. When I was told that I would never be able to buy more properties when my portfolio was worth $4 million, I didn't believe it, and I went and found a mortgage broker who could help me. Now, of course, my portfolio is valued at $20 million.

One of the most valuable resources that each one of us has is time as it is a finite resource. This means that you must maximise the time you have available to you by outsourcing things that can be completed more cheaply by someone else, such as cleaning your house, or to experts who have more experience than you and who can help you achieve your goals more quickly.

## Principle 4: Make leverage your superpower

Leverage is generally the reason why some people become rich and others don't. The wealthy are not afraid to leverage other people's money (the banks, for example) to purchase more assets.

By making leverage your superpower, you will be able to multiply your returns on income, which will create additional income streams for you over the long term. Fundamentally, you must understand the difference between good debt (such as mortgages) that can make you more money and bad debt (such as personal loans) that will make you poorer.

Another of the secrets to financial success is using phantom equity, which is the equity that has grown in your assets over time. You can recycle phantom equity into other assets that then grow in value, creating more phantom equity. It becomes a perfect money snowball over time.

## Principle 5: Tolerate and manage risk

By now, you know that I have a higher tolerance for risk than most people because I used to skydive for fun and was a freight train driver for a number of years as well. However, everyone can increase their risk profile through education and better financial literacy. You can also tolerate and manage risk by adopting a business mindset when it comes to your investment strategies and financial dreams.

Managing risk should involve understanding how risky certain investment vehicles are – with real estate being the lowest risk, in my opinion – as well as learning how to ignore the media scaremongering that tends to happen when markets are softening temporarily.

Remember, it doesn't matter what prices are doing today or tomorrow; what matters is what they are doing in 10 or 20 years' time!

## Principle 6: Create compounding wealth

Most people who invest in real estate in particular give up after about five years. Why do you think that is? Well, it's either because they bought the wrong properties or because they were speculating.

History has shown us time and time again that it takes time for most people to grow significant wealth – even Warren Buffett was 60 by the time he made his first $1 billion. That is why you must be persistent and patient as you diligently work towards retiring younger and richer.

Over the years – it could take a decade or two, or even three – you will be creating an investment portfolio, potentially across a variety of asset classes, that will provide multiple income streams for you, plus the benefits of value uplifts over time.

However, don't forget to enjoy the fruits of your labour along the way (within reason) so that you give yourself the best chance to see your wealth creation journey through to the end.

By adopting these techniques, you can develop your own money blueprint and change your financial life – and the lives of the generations that come after you, too!

## Where to from here?

Now it's time to put all of these principles into practice. You may need to read this book a couple of times and make notes along the way – whatever you need to do to set yourself on the path to retire younger and richer!

Of course, feel free to reach out to me anytime if you have questions about any of the concepts that I have outlined in this book. My overarching goal is to help as many people as possible achieve financial success during their lifetimes, just as I have done.

Throughout this book, I have often also referenced my Mastery courses, which I developed to help anyone learn how to build real compounding wealth through strategic property buying – but without the hype or the smoke and mirrors! So far, more than 1200 people from all walks of life have completed the course. Here is some feedback from our students:

'While it is hard to break out of a traditional mindset, I am living proof it can happen! Since I started learning about investing and mindset, I have received two large pay rises at work as my employers are absolutely blown away with how hard I've been working. I owe this all to this course, which has shifted my mindset.' – *Alyise*

'The lessons are explained simply enough for me to understand as someone who is new to investing, but are also really detailed with a lot of value to give. The videos are super motivating as well and make you feel it is all within reach. Game changer!' – *Brendan*

By heading to yourpropertyyourwealth.com.au you will find not only more information on the courses but also lots of useful knowledge that you can use to continue your investment education.

Thank you for entrusting me to help you achieve your financial goal of retiring younger and richer. I truly believe that by following the six principles outlined in my book, you have every opportunity to turn your financial dreams into reality!

If you got value out of this book, please leave a review online, either with an online bookseller such as Amazon or in a social media post. This will help get the word out there so more people can retire younger and richer.

Now, my ambitious friends, it is time to take action.

# Glossary

**Abundance mindset:** The belief that you have the time and resources necessary to accomplish your goals. Compare with *scarcity mindset*.

**Amortisation:** The process of paying off a debt through regular payments.

**Angel investors:** Wealthy individuals who provide seed money for startup businesses.

**Assets:** Possessions, which may be expected to increase in value (such as property or shares) or lose value (such as cars).

**Break-even point:** The point at which your income covers your costs. Anything beyond this point is profit.

**Burner properties:** Properties that you keep in your portfolio temporarily to generate equity through capital growth, which you then use to pay down the debt on the rest of your portfolio. They are effective because, as long as you choose the right properties, they can grow in value much faster than you can save your active income.

**Capital growth:** The appreciation in value of an asset over time.

**Cash flow:** Money coming in or out; that is, income versus expenses. If more money is coming in than going out, that's *positive cash flow*; if more money is going out than coming in, that's *negative cash flow*.

**Compounding:** A powerful investing concept that involves earning returns on both your original investment and on returns you received previously. For compounding to work, you need to reinvest your returns back into your account.

**Consolidation:** The process of shoring up your investments by increasing cash buffers and paying down debt while your assets increase in value.

**Cryptocurrency:** A type of digital currency that allows people to make direct payments to one another through an online system. Compare with *fiat currencies*.

**Debt:** Borrowed money, which generally accrues interest at a rate set by the lender. *Bad debt* is debt taken out to purchase an asset that is not likely to increase in value, such as a car. *Good debt* is debt taken out to purchase an asset that *is* likely to increase in value, such as a property or shares.

**Debt multiples:** The ratio of total debt to EBITDA.

**Depreciation:** An accounting method that determines the decrease in an asset's value over time. With property, you can claim tax back on the depreciation of certain assets such as carpets, curtains or appliances.

**Diversification:** Spreading your investments across different asset classes.

**EBITDA:** Earnings before interest, taxes, depreciation and amortisation. This indicates a portfolio's performance.

**Emergency fund:** A cash reserve set aside for unplanned expenses, such as home repairs, medical bills or loss of income.

**Equity:** The difference between the current value of an asset (such as a property) and how much you owe on it. *Phantom equity* is my term for equity in an asset that you bought using equity in the first place, so you never put any money that you had to work for into the asset.

**Fiat currencies:** Government-issued currencies not backed by a commodity such as gold or silver. Compare with *cryptocurrency*.

**Generational wealth:** Assets passed down from one generation of a family to another.

**Inflation:** The increase in prices, or the erosion of real value, over time.

**Interest rate:** The price paid for borrowing money, expressed as a percentage over a period of time (for example, 5 per cent per annum over 30 years). A *fixed interest rate* never changes, whereas a *variable interest rate* may move higher or lower over time.

**Lenders:** Entities that lend money that you must then pay back, usually with interest. They include banks as well as nonbank entities.

**Leverage:** The use of debt to amplify investment returns.

**Liabilities:** Things that you owe to other parties, such as personal loans.

**Lifestyle inflation:** An increase in spending in line with an increase in income.

**Liquidity:** The speed at which an asset can be bought or sold. Liquid assets (such as shares) can be bought and sold relatively quickly and cheaply, whereas illiquid assets (such as property) are more expensive and time-consuming to buy and sell.

**Loan-to-value ratio (LVR):** A ratio showing the size of a loan relative to the value of the asset the loan is being used to buy. It is expressed as a percentage; for example, an LVR of 80 per cent means that the loan is 80 per cent of the value of the asset.

**Manifestation:** The process of visualising to alter your perception of a situation to make your goal feel more achievable.

**Money blueprint:** A plan that you can follow to repeat the process of wealth accumulation.

**Mortgage:** A type of loan used to purchase or maintain a piece of real estate. The borrower agrees to pay the lender over time, and the property then serves as collateral to secure the loan.

**Net worth:** The total wealth of an individual, household or company, taking all financial assets and liabilities into account.

**Novated lease:** A lease for a car whereby the obligations in the contract have been transferred from one party to another, such as your employer. For example, your employer might take money directly from your pre-tax salary to make repayments on the lease.

**Passive income:** Money you did not have to trade your time to earn, such as rental income from an investment property.

**Personal loans:** A loan that does not require collateral or security. Personal loans are often used to purchase things like holidays or assets that are not expected to increase in value over time, such as cars.

**Principal:** The initial amount invested, or the total amount borrowed from a lender.

**Purchasing power:** The value of a currency expressed in terms of the number of goods or services a unit of that currency can buy.

**Rentvestors:** Property investors who rent out the property (or properties) they own while living in a rental property themselves, often so they can live in an area in which they cannot afford to buy.

**Return on investment:** A ratio of the net profit of an investment over its total cost.

**Scarcity mindset:** The belief that your time and resources are limited, which causes you to place limits on your goals. Compare with *abundance mindset*.

**Serviceability:** A lender's assessment of your ability to meet repayments on a loan.

**Side hustle:** Work you take on outside of your primary job for the purpose of supplementing your income.

**Torrens title:** A land title whereby you are the sole owner of both the land and the building on it. This is opposed to a *strata title*, whereby some areas, such as driveways or the roofs of adjoining properties, are shared.

**Yield:** The income returned on an investment, usually expressed as a percentage per annum.

# References

Australian Bureau of Statistics, 'Average weekly earnings, Australia', 17 August 2023, <abs.gov.au/statistics/labour/earnings-and-working-conditions/average-weekly-earnings-australia/may-2023>.

Singapore Management University Lee Kong Chian School of Business, 'How to beat the third-generation curse', accessed 27 September 2023, <business.smu.edu.sg/master-wealth-management/lkcsb-community/how-beat-third-generation-curse>.

C Clarey, 'Olympians use imagery as mental training', *The New York Times*, 22 February 2014, <nytimes.com/2014/02/23/sports/olympics/olympians-use-imagery-as-mental-training.html>.

D Pereira, 'Is Tesla profitable?', *The Business Model Analyst*, 16 March 2023, <businessmodelanalyst.com/is-tesla-profitable/>.

Trading Economics, 'Australia inflation rate', accessed 27 September 2023, <tradingeconomics.com/australia/inflation-cpi>.

P Vincent, 'Incredible classified ads from 1972 show Sydneysiders could buy a three-bedroom terrace in the inner suburbs for just SIX PER CENT of what it would cost now while a family home with ocean views was a tenth of the price', *The Daily Mail*, 21 July 2021, <dailymail.co.uk/news/ article-9808217/Classified-ads-1972-Sydneysiders-buy-three-bedroom-city-terrace-10-000.html>.

CoreLogic, *Aussie Progress Report*, March 2022, <assets.ctfassets.net/nbklqgdg5mdx/37IPbmPPrNgpgo WkSIfN3m/1c5b7635895a20936a4da3cca49cc0de/Aussie_ Progress_Report_FINAL__1_.pdf>.

G Bullock, 'Rates: 1990 versus 2007', *9News*, 15 August 2007, <9news.com.au/finance/rates-1990-versus-2007/8251875f-a878-49a5-bca6-559d2dcdb361>.

# Index

# About the author

Daniel Walsh began investing in property at just 19 years of age, when he was earning just $34,000 a year, and has since built an impressive property portfolio worth $20 million. He has been featured by high-profile media outlets such as *9News*, *Domain*, *Business Insider*, news.com.au and *The Mentor with Mark Bouris* for his success with property investment.

His passion for real estate and wealth creation led him to found Your Property Your Wealth, an award-winning buyer's agency, with his wife Sophie. Your Property Your Wealth helps clients build wealth through property investing so that they can ultimately achieve financial freedom. Your Property Your Wealth also provides investment education through its Mastery courses. Daniel's aim is to create a community of the top one per cent of investors in Australia.

**Be better with business books**

**MAJOR STREET**

We hope you enjoy reading this book. We'd love you to post a review on social media or your favourite bookseller site. Please include the hashtag #majorstreetpublishing.

Major Street Publishing specialises in business, leadership, personal finance and motivational non-fiction books. If you'd like to receive regular updates about new Major Street books, email info@majorstreet.com.au and ask to be added to our mailing list.

Visit majorstreet.com.au to find out more about our books (print, audio and ebooks) and authors, read reviews and find links to our Your Next Read podcast.

We'd love you to follow us on social media.

in linkedin.com/company/major-street-publishing

f facebook.com/MajorStreetPublishing

○ instagram.com/majorstreetpublishing

🐦 @MajorStreetPub